HUDDERSFIELD
IN OLD PHOTOGRAPHS
A SECOND SELECTION

Happy Days — to you
Hazel Wheeler

HUDDERSFIELD
IN OLD PHOTOGRAPHS
A SECOND SELECTION

—— COLLECTED BY ——
HAZEL WHEELER

ALAN SUTTON

Alan Sutton Publishing Limited
Phoenix Mill · Far Thrupp · Stroud · Gloucestershire

First Published 1990

British Library Cataloguing in Publication Data

Huddersfield in old photographs: a second selection.
1. West Yorkshire (Metropolitan County). Huddersfield,
history
I. Wheeler, H. (Hazel)
942.813

ISBN 0–86299–848–4

Typeset in 9/10 Korinna.
Typesetting and origination by
Alan Sutton Publishing Limited.
Printed in Great Britain by
Dotesios Printers Limited.

CONTENTS

MARKET PLACE, Huddersfield. In 1901 gentlemen's hairdresser and umbrella maker, George North, traded in Market Place. The entrance was in the passage next to Mr A. Morton's Dining Rooms. He was also a dealer in combs, brushes, and all 'toilet requisites,' and sold 'Cigars of the Choicest Brands'.

INTRODUCTION

This second volume of old photographs in and around Huddersfield recalls the minutiae of life in the district. Many of the scenes would now be forgotten, were it not for the good sense and sentimentality of those who hoarded treasures that others dismissed as 'a load of old junk'. Newspapers reflect national events as they affect our town, but many of the snaps in this book have formerly only been seen by the immediate families and friends of people featured. What enjoyment can be gained by listening to the stories connected with them! – to be reminded of the coronation of King George VI and Queen Elizabeth in 1937, for example, when flags could be bought for a penny, house flags for 9d. Whitfields of Ramsden Street advertised in the *Examiner*, 'Book Your Seat Now for the Coronation, 1s. 11d. a week, – listen in on the Philco wireless sets'. Jarratt, Pyrah and Armitage announced that they, timber merchants, had flagpoles of any length.

Old Huddersfield citizens look back with affection to the old cobbled Pack Horse Yard. Barron's Craftworkers Supply Stores there had meat safes, clothes posts, rustic arches, and similar almost forgotten household articles for sale.

In the latter years of the nineteenth century Mrs W.H. Shaw of Meadow Farm, Farnley Tyas, advertised 'Teas and Refreshment Provided in Nice Style. Good

Stabling. Choice Cigars and Mineral Waters. Good Piano'. A rural haven indeed.

In September 1896 several cases of hydrophobia arose, as a result of bites from mad dogs. John Blackburn of Fieldhouse, Leeds Road, also lost several cows which had been bitten by a dog. Some aspects of living change little – if not mad cows, mad dogs. However, the cost of living has changed. The Cash Supply Stores, 33 New Street, offered 'Force, the New Food', at 6d. a packet, 'Grand Tea for the kitchen' 1s. 8d. per lb, 'Palethorpes Celebrated Fife sausages, fresh every day', and 'Whiskey, 3s. 6d. a bottle'.

On 19 April 1932 an early morning fire at the Grand Picture House was discovered by a postman. Subsequently he was presented with a life pass for his promptitude in giving the alarm. It was fortunate for him that cinemas were then at the height of popularity. The following year saw the opening of the Regent Cinema, designed by Mr J.H. Freer, of Fenay Bridge. *Cavalcade* was the first film shown, admission costing: 1s. 9d., 1s. 3d. or 6d. In 1946 war and glamour films began to give way to stories about more down-to-earth people. On 18 May scenes were shot at Marsden for *The Crowthers of Bankdam*. Things began to change for the worse when, on 11 September that year, Huddersfield Town Council Watch Committee attended a performance of *The Mad Ghoul*, a horror film, at the Picturedrome.

At the end of February 1933, after a continuous forty-eight-hour snowfall, the 'Great Blizzard' came to an end. Households had been without milk for three or four days. The clearing of snow, which took nearly a week, at a cost of £7,000, gave many of the unemployed a strenuous job. An aeroplane was forced down at Sheepridge on the first day of the snowfall, and a press photographer passenger had to continue his journey by train.

Life was never dull for some in the town. In April that year a passer-by was soberly going about his business on Queen Street, when he nonchalantly walked over a manhole. At exactly that moment there was a build up of gas, and an explosion occurred. The manhole lid, made of concrete in a massive iron frame, rose in the air to a height of between 30 and 40 ft. The noise was heard over a large area, and the pedestrian had to be taken into the County Court Rooms to recover.

During the First World War, Hirst's Clog Shop was at 13 Northgate. They guaranteed, after seeing the shape of the foot, to make an easy fitting clog, cheap, warm and comfortable. More than boot comfort at less cost. All clog soles were hand-made. 'Try a pair for use in Garden or Wash-Kitchen' they suggested. How strange the streets must have been, when, shrouded in deep drifts of snow, the sound of workers' clogs were muffled as mill chimneys hooted.

Back in 1875–6, when a covered market was first discussed, Alderman D. Sykes stated that Huddersfield was 'the dearest town in the Kingdom', a matter which Council and Chamber of Trade should urgently consider. Prices for potatoes, apples, and onions were from 25 to 40 per cent higher than in Leeds, and a good market hall would alter things. Did it do so? Some still consider the town more expensive than its neighbours.

However, home is home, wherever you go. One thing about living in Huddersfield, almost inconceivable happenings are never hard to find. Never more so than at funerals. It was on 26 March 1869 that, in Aldmondbury cemetery, mourners were standing round the open grave, earth being shovelled on to the coffin, when three distinct knocks were heard. The digger flung down his shovel.

Blank alarm gave way to urgent commands. 'Send for the carpenter . . .' Canon Hulbert immediately ordered the burial to be stopped. The young carpenter unscrewed the lid, but none could induce him to remove it, so the grave digger did so. According to the workman, the poor man lay inside, as cold as marble, and far less disturbed than the gathering crowd, 'in his little home'.

'He looks very comfortable,' pronounced the grave digger, and ordered the lid to be screwed down for a second time. His vivid imagination – and who would not have one in such an occupation – had led him to believe the sounds were emerging from the inside of the coffin. It simply had not found its proper level when the earth landed on it, causing it to creak three times. How relieved those present must have been when seated at last round a groaning table of ham, pickles, tea, and bread and butter, leaving the creaking coffin and its occupant to their eternal rest.

If the funeral tea had been at the Lion Restaurant in the Station Square central tram terminus, Huddersfield, they would have patronized an establishment that boasted 'Dinners, Teas, Luncheons. Ladies' Dining Rooms. Ladies' and Gentlemen's Lavatories. Smoke Room.'

Of course any repast can only be properly enjoyed if teeth are in good order. Mr A.F. Hughes of 7 Chapel Hill, in the early years of the century, advertised 'Durable, Natural, and Unsurpassable false teeth. On Vulcanite, Platina, and Gold Mountings. Painless extractions, with or without gas. Hours 9.00–7.30 p.m.'

When we look back to earlier years, we find Huddersfield people were as upset about rising prices as they are today. Bottled beer, in February 1916, was up by $\frac{1}{2}$d. and bakers put up the 'family loaf' by $\frac{1}{2}$d.

But we can always close our eyes to what we dislike in the present day by opening them to old photographs, and stories of days gone by. They are one of the most therapeutic medicines anyone can devise – and it does not even have to be bought in 1s. 3d. bottles from Henry Sykes, chemists, or Needhams of Buxton Road. Or, do as John O'Hara's father did when his wife left him in 1935, after he habitually returned home 'blotto' from the Elephant and Castle. When a fortnight had passed, Winnie decided that he had been punished enough. Back she and the children came from her mother's in Barnsley, expecting a tearful reunion. However, her husband was merrily singing 'We'll make a Bonfire of our Troubles' as he washed up in the stone sink. She hit him with the rolling pin and departed again . . . but they thought the world of each other really.

Perhaps we ought to make a bonfire of our troubles too, but do make sure that any old photographs don't go on it, won't you?

Town and District

WESTGATE, HUDDERSFIELD. Prince Charles would approve of the architecture in Westgate Many years ago the old Cherry Tree Inn was a landmark in that area. Cooper, Webb & Son Ltd, provision merchants, traded where the horse and cart are. In the thirties W.H. Dawson & Sons at 14–16 Westgate sold exclusive men's wear. A tailored business suit cost between £4 10s. and £9 10s. Smartly dressed citizens, especially ladies, met for afternoon tea and morning coffee either in Sylvio's or Whiteley's cafés, to be served by waitresses in black dresses, starched white collars and cuffs, and little frilly white aprons.

Market Square. Huddersfield.

MARKET SQUARE. The town was smart when this photograph was taken. No litter in the streets, good quality clothes in the shops, and people not bothered about owning cars because trams were cheap, frequent, and reliable. Rushworths high class shop was the building on the corner, with sun blinds down. The most oft said 'farewell' in those days was not 'see you later' but, 'I'll see you at Rushworths corner...'

BEAUMONT'S OPTICIANS. Ernest Beaumont started the business in Lindley before moving for a short time to Lion Chambers, St George's Square. They moved to 2 New Street in 1908, where they still are. The front of the practice was altered in 1961. This photograph was taken about 1920, when the style for glasses would be rimless frames, tortoiseshell frames, steel and gold rims, monocles, pince-nez and lorgnettes, all of them very much smaller frames than those of today. Some examples of the 1920 frames are retained, and occasionally loaned to dramatic societies. Seventy years ago the cost of a pair of glasses was about £1 10s., and 5s. for a sight test.

Below, left:
LADIES WALKING ON NEW STREET, SHOPPING. A typical New Street scene around 1930. Sisters Fanny Robinson and Clara Armitage stroll along, arm in arm. Rolled umbrellas and smart hats were everyday wear for shopping in town. 'Light' music was enjoyable in the thirties. J. Wood and Sons Ltd, music dealers, had premises on New Street. Pianos were 'in go' and more than one family always had a musical evening after the weekly baking day was over.

Huddersfield Co-operative Society, Ltd. Central Offices and Stores

HUDDERSFIELD CO-OPERATIVE SOCIETY. The construction of the main Co-op building was started in 1880 and the entire block completed in 1894. An extension was completed and opened in 1937 and at the same time the older premises were modernized internally. Many families relied on the Co-op 'divvy' to buy new clothes for Whitsuntide, or to finance 'Wakes' week holidays. Nowadays the premises front on to a pedestrian precinct. The architect of the original building was Joseph Berry.

THE GENERAL POST OFFICE. In 1850 Huddersfield Post Office was at 49 New Street, with Mr William Moore as the postmaster. In early years letters could be placed in a post-box fixed to tram cars. It is strange to recall that stamps remained at a halfpenny to send a postcard for years, and local items would be certain of being delivered the same day. The present GPO is down Northumberland Street. The old post office building (1874/5) was constructed at a cost of £11,000. Telegraph boys at the post office were known as 'Penny Runners'. Originally the space in front of this building was suggested for the site of the Town Hall.

HUDDERSFIELD HAD NO TRAMWAYS until 1882, though it was one of the first boroughs to operate a tramway system. The first routes opened in 1882 were worked by horse-drawn trams for a few years. Then trams hauled by steam engines made their appearance in 1883, lasting for eighteen years until the conversion of all routes to electronic traction. Trams also provided a means of advertising. Here, 'Zebra' grate polish has pride of place on a tram heading for Crosland Moor. The last tram to Brighouse ran in 1940.

EARLY POLICE STATION. In 1898 the police station, along with the public library and art gallery, was opened. The early police headquarters on Peel Street have been replaced by the new Market Hall which was opened in 1970. A new police station opened in 1967. On 14 December 1896 landlord John Garthwaite was charged with keeping the Beaumont Arms open during unlawful hours. However, magistrates thought it only right that those attending funerals should have a place in which to shelter. Mr Heaton, Chief Constable, said there was not a better conducted house in the country. The case was dismissed.

MARKET WALK IN THE SIXTIES. Whiteley's of Westgate also had a confectionery business on Market Walk. They were an old established firm when the town was incorporated, the first Mr Whiteley purchasing what was already, even then, an established business. Their vanilla slices were scrumptious! In 1909 a Whiteley's wedding cake cost from half a guinea. Another long established firm on Market Walk is Fillans, jewellers. Caroline Wheeler waits with wicker basket in foreground.

POLICEMEN ON VICTORIA LANE in the 1960s. The site of the former market hall, which was opened in 1880. Broken dolls used to have their fragile bodies mended at a dolls' hospital on Victoria Lane. A popular old pub, the Albert, at the far end of the street, opened its doors to its first customers in 1878. Blackburn's Art Florists also traded on Victoria Lane.

ERNEST ASQUITH'S GROCERY SHOP on Kidroyd Lane, off Aldmondbury Bank. Like all such shops, it was a meeting place for all. Note the boy playing on a 'trolley cart' coming down the hill. Old pram wheels and a piece of rope to steer them with were ideal for making these. Back in 1868 a 4 lb loaf cost 7½d., ten cigarettes 'a tanner', cheese was 7d. per lb, cocoa 3d. per ½lb, ham (1lb) 1s. How cheaply a Christmas cake could be baked, with currants 1s. for 2 lbs, raisins also 1s., sultanas 1s. 6d. for 2 lb, almonds 9d. a ¼lb, mixed peel 10d. for ½lb. A stone of flour cost 2s. 1d. Even at the time of the photograph customers had to take their own containers for eggs, treacle, cheese, lard, sugar, tea and other goods which were weighed out in the shop. Signs outside Asquith's included Brooke Bond Tea, Hudson's Soap, and Sugden's Flour.

ANOTHER GROUP OF CHILDREN congregated around Asquith's shop. One boy is holding a 'booler' — some were made of wood, others of iron; a stick guided their way down the streets. In those pre-First-World-War days the weights and measures man used to make spot checks on grocery stores, to make sure they were not giving short weight. In the 1920s Miss Mellor's collop shop was further on the road. She was nicknamed 'Polly Collop' and sold collops at eight for 2d.

RAVENSKNOWLE ROAD, MOLDGREEN. This is typical of the rows of terraced houses in the area. Children sat on the stone walls to chat. Dashing into the road after a horse and cart had gone by to scoop up manure for the garden was a common pastime, as was fishing in dustbins for old cans to play 'Tin Can Squat'. Chalking hopscotch on pavements was a good game too, as was skipping. In those days it was safe enough to play football or cricket in the roads, when only the occasional horse and cart lumbered past.

WOODSOME HALL GOLF CLUB. Woodsome takes its name from extensive woodlands which lie west of the hall. In a nearby field the Woodsome Flower Show used to take place. In 1586 John Kaye left the mansion house at Woodsome to his eldest son Robert. A flint axe was once discovered where the carriage drive terminates in the high road, proving the prehistoric past of the area.

FARNLEY LINE. On 5 December 1916, Major Holliday's 'shooting day' at Farnley Tyas was a big day. In the excitement of discussion J.F. Eastwood, landlord of the Golden Cock served liquid refreshments to four visitors out of hours. For this lapse he was fined £5 and the imbibers £1 each. The hostelry is now named Farnley Cock. The area provides a delightful walk, with bluebells in springtime, and an abundance of blackberries in Autumn.

FENAY HALL, built in 1605 by Nicholas Fenay. The hall was built with tunnels leading to the village church and nearby Castle Hill. The Fenay family were stewards of Wakefield Manor, the local courts, and they used to ride over and fine people for not cutting their lawns and similar offences. One owner of the hall discovered brasses from the church in the attic, dating perhaps from the time of the Reformation.

Thunder Bridge near Kirkburton

THUNDER BRIDGE, KIRKBURTON. The Woodman inn is situated in this pretty district. Smoke curling out of one of the chimneys indicates this picture was taken before the smokeless zone came into operation. Storthes Hall Hospital, not far from here, had the Revd Joseph Ogden as Free Church chaplain for nine years. A 'Stay and Corset' mill opened on 22 January 1876 in Kirkburton. A couple of years later Amos Tinker, cart driver employed by dyer David Lockwood, Kirkburton, was buried in the churchyard on 28 April. The hearse was drawn by the deceased man's horse. On the following Monday morning the horse itself was dead in its stable.

BOG HALL, KIRKHEATON. The home of Wilfred Rhodes, cricketer, born at Kirkheaton in 1877, capped for England in 1899. Nobody ever approached his total of 4,187 wickets. Wilfred went to school in Hopton, then worked on the railway at Mirfield. When duties finished at half past two he ran all the way back to make sure of a game of cricket. One Saturday he rang the 'knocking off' bell at 1.30 p.m. in order to get to the match. That ended his railway career. In 1915 the greatest honour that had come to the club was that two of Kirkheaton's young men became known among England's finest cricketers.

THE OLD CLOUGH HOUSE. Halifax Old Road is on the site of Clough House today. It was demolished in 1899. The drawing-room was known as the Ghost Room. When a death occurred in the house, bodies were placed in coffins there. Abraham Firth of Clough House shot himself on 22 November 1769 after being at Aldmondbury Pig Fair. Ann Firth died in 1795 (she married Thomas Macaulay) and thus Clough House Estates devolved upon her descendants. Next to the coachhouse was a barn, and a carriage drawn by two ponies attracted and amused local children. There were croquet and tennis courts in the grounds, and mulberrry, fig and walnut trees in the gardens. Peacocks and peahens used to roost in the trees above the road. On Christmas Eve brass bands played hymns and carols in front of Clough House. On 14 September 1819 a fire burnt down the old barn and livestock was burnt to death. Some were buried in a field below the house called Tan Yard Ing — now Norman Park. One cow was called Old Stick-in-the-mud, because it often wandered into boggy places and stuck fast.

A PRE-FIRST-WORLD-WAR PHOTOGRAPH of the old well at the top of Whitacre Street, Deighton. The four stone stumps made excellent seats for young men and their girls enjoying a spot of 'courting'. The gas lamp was a useful addition too. Crawshaw's shop and post office was on the right-hand side going up Deighton Road.

DEIGHTON AGAIN, before the wars. Once known as 'the prettiest village in the district' before the estates were built in the 1930s over the 'Ridings' — fields where generations of children played cricket and football. Tom and Muriel Jessop still live at No. 90, celebrating a Golden Wedding, fifty years of wedded bliss in the same house, in June 1990. Many will recall Tom when he was a plumber at Garten's, before having his own business.

THE SHEEPRIDGE TO DEIGHTON ROAD. Providence Chapel is on the right of the photograph, and Oddy's fish and chip shop is on the opposite side. The sign on the left, behind the lamp-post, says 'Thomas Smart'. Warrenfield, further down the road on the right-hand side, became an ARP post during the Second World War. The Sheepridge Laundry Co. was acquired by Mr Lawrence Batley in 1958 for his 'cash and carry' business, before being demolished in 1963 in a road improvement scheme. Old locals fancifully nicknamed the area 'Chelsea'.

Keeper's Cottage, Butternab.

THOMAS HIND, HUDDERSFIELD.

BUTTERNAB, CROSLAND MOOR, home of the Colne Valley Beagles. It is traditional for a hunt to take place on Boxing Day, and the 'sound of the horn' can often be heard by those in the vicinity. The workhouse used to be at Crosland Moor. On 16 July 1917 the assistant there received a wage increase from £40 to £60 though away on military service.

COSY NOOK, GRIMSCAR. The Romans built a tile kiln in Grimscar wood, and during their occupation probably traded with the local inhabitants, who used Roman coins as well as their own. On 3 November 1915 a two-day sale of work in aid of clearing the debt on St Cuthbert's church, Grimscar, was opened by Mrs Holdich, and £344 was raised.

STORTHES HALL, KIRKBURTON. Set in a pretty wooded district, the asylum has been home to many. Now it is in the process of being vacated, as are so many other institutions. Families visiting used to talk about 'going to Burton', not to the hospital. The Storthes appear frequently as principals or witnesses in ancient charters connected with the district. The earliest mention is of Matthew de Storthes in the reign of Henry III.

The Lake, Beaumont Park

HUDDERSFIELD

THE LAKE IN BEAUMONT PARK is no more. A trip to Beaumont Park helped pass many a school holiday when a family could not afford to go to the seaside. Small boats could be sailed on the lake, and a child could almost believe he or she was at the seaside. Ducks can be seen round the tree in the photograph.

THE WALK, BEAUMONT PARK, HUDDERSFIELD

THE WALK, BEAUMONT PARK. Prettily lined with colourful trees and shrubs The Walk was for the more sedate. The bowler-hatted gentleman in the photograph takes the air and rests on one of the many seats provided. Beaumont Park is an area of natural beauty.

ALDMONDBURY BANK. Moldgreen Conservative Club is one of the buildings on the left side of the photograph. In the old cottages lived a character the local children named 'Nanny Greenteeth' in the 1930s. Bankside Mill was in the area, and children frequently fell into its dam.

THE BEAUMONT ARMS, KIRKHEATON, photographed in the 1960s. In 1902 there was a court case concerning a couple of men who were found carrying a large can across to the church. When police examined it, they found a gallon of hot ale and rum. 'Something for the bell ringers', explained Edgar Carter. It had, apparently, been a recognized custom to give beer to them on New Year's Eve, there being no place in the belfry for warming up the beer if they got it there before 11 o'clock. Carter, of Lepton, said they went round for subscriptions at New Year, and the defendant gave beer instead of money. The bench dismissed the summons as it was an old custom – 'but it appeared to be sailing rather near the wind'.

LINDLEY TOWER. This familiar landmark is on the opposite side of the street to the English Card Clothing Company, and near to the Huddersfield Infirmary. The tower was erected by James Nield Sykes JP, of Field Head, Lindley, for the benefit of the inhabitants of his native village in 1902. Lindley boasted the famous 'Wappy Stout' made from spring water at Wapping Spring Brewery on Lindley Moor. In the First World War, Lindley Parish Room workers, at a cost of nearly £100 for material, made 5,300 sandbags for soldiers.

LINTHWAITE in the 1960s. Linthwaite church is in the distance. It is an area of spectacular views, where bilberries may be gathered on the hillsides in summertime. Locals used to refer to the area as 'Linfit'. In the 1860s on the north side of Linfit Fold was a spout; on the south side was a well near the old Toll Bar, known as the Bar Well. The Bar Well retained a wonderful supply of good water all year round, and was patronized by inhabitants far distant, when ordinary supplies failed them. Though that from the spout was not as reliable in quantity, some favoured its taste. The tale goes that a chap ordered his son 'Tak that can, and fetch me some thra' t'spaet.' The lad went instead to the nearer Bar Well. When his father took a draught he exclaimed 'that's the watter, there's nothing like t'spaet' (spout).

TRYING TO WALK ON COBBLED TOMMY LANE, Linthwaite, is Elizabeth Wheeler, in the mid-sixties. Certainly not the place for high-heeled shoes. On 2 October 1915, a Belgian repatriation hut, costing £60, and collected by Linthwaite Women's Liberal Association, plus £20 granted by the Repatriation Society was erected near Black Rock, and christened 'Linthwaite'.

ANOTHER PART OF RUGGED LINTHWAITE in the sixties. Rough dark dry stone walls, outhouses, and washing blowing in the clear moorland air characterize the area. A murder took place at the Ivy Inn, Linthwaite, on 21 August 1891. Catherine Dennis, aged sixteen, was murdered by James Stockwell, who was hanged in Armley Jail on 5 January 1892. A tombstone was erected by the public as a token of respect for the young girl.

COWLERSLEY, with a view towards Crosland Moor. Elizabeth and Caroline Wheeler playing by the stream with cousin Shirley Taylor (centre) in the 1960s. Modern houses are now built there, with the stream running at the bottom of their gardens. Crosland Moor golf links are 'up on the tops.'

BLACKMOORFOOT RESERVOIR. The steady growth of Huddersfield necessitated an additional water supply. Deer Hill reservoir was brought into use in 1875 and Blackmoorfoot the following year.

LONGWOOD. The Society of Friends, whose benevolent activities aroused senseless opposition, were active in Huddersfield before 1770, when their first meeting house was built at Longwood. The first Methodist church there was built in 1837. In about 1825, a Sunday School began in a cottage on Lamb Hall Road. Longwood is known for its 'Sing'; Haigh's skep and basket makers to the textile industry since 1828 and Joseph Hoyle's of Prospect Mills, woollen and worsted manufacturers since 1865.

HEPWORTH VILLAGE. During the plague in London a quantity of wearing apparel had been sent to Foster Place, a farmhouse near Hepworth, occupied by the Beaver family. The clothing had belonged to a relative who had died in London. After its arrival the family were suddenly taken ill and died, those attending them also. The plague then raged violently in the district. Inhabitants at the north-west end of the village cut off all communication with their infected neighbours, erecting a strong hedge or fence across the highway and so that part was saved. The dead were interred in a field adjoining the village. Hepworth gave name to the family of Adam de Hepworth in 1333, who held lands in Huddersfield. A branch of the family settled in Shepley. Hepworth has bold, diversified scenery.

COOK'S STUDY, HOLMFIRTH. An ARP post during the Second World War. Cook's Study was built by Sir John Spencer Stanhope of Cannon Hall in 1852 on the wild Cartworth moorlands above Holmfirth. Some used to cut peat round about here for fuel.

HONLEY BRIDGE. Buses going to Hope Bank turned round at Honley. Honley Feast used to be a highlight of the year with 'open house' for all comers. There was Wombwell's Menagerie, Pablo's Circus, a wild travelling theatre, marionette shows, pea saloons, flying boxes, and waxworks, as well as human and animal curiosities hidden in tents. Walls were covered with boards filled with sheets of printed song ballads, accounts of sensational murders, and other items tending to excite horror. Children were given a penny, with grave warnings not to be 'spendthrifts'. Barrels of 'home-brewed', huge pieces of roast beef, veal and fruit pies, were all available. The place was transformed with caravans, elephants and camels.

KING'S MILL LANE, ASPLEY. Home of weaving sheds and Kaye's mill which specialized in making 'Kayso' aprons which sold for about 2s. 11d. It was a boast of King's Mill Lane, at one time, that there had never been an accident there; it was so narrow that drivers were extra careful. A Huddersfield lady who worked at another clothing firm, Wilson's Bespoke Tailors in St George's Square, earned 6s. 8d. a week in 1939 when aged fourteen. Her hours were 8 a.m. to 6 p.m. and 8–12 noon Saturdays. At the time, better-off clients paid up to 25 guineas to have a suit made.

ISLE OF SKYE HOTEL. Like Nont Sarah's, an out-of-the-way beauty spot visited in days gone by, it was a coaching inn with primitive amenities. Outside lavatories, tubs, no water or electricity laid on. Oil lamps were the means of lighting the place. Owned by Bentley and Shaw Brewery, the Isle of Skye Hotel was closed on 31 October 1956, and demolished August 1958. In the photograph the waitresses are wearing long white aprons. Dry stone walling surrounds the building. It is 1,477 ft above sea-level on the Meltham and Marsden moors. It was popular with hikers, who did not mind the stone floors. There used to be a well outside to pump water.

SECTION TWO

The First World War

HUDDERSFIELD in a Tank.

MANY WERE THE MILITARY HONOURS heaped upon those from Huddersfield during the First World War. Among those on the roll of honour are James Sallis, nineteen, killed while tending the wounded, and twenty-year-old Fred Singleton, killed by a shell while carrying rations. On 19 September 1915 First Class Air Mechanic, Irvin Shaw, formerly employed at Clayton's Karrier Car Co., went in an aeroplane with Lieutenant Powell on patrol, and at 9,000 and 6,000 ft up fought with two Taubes (German machines) and destroyed them. Huddersfield attracted the attention of the enemy through being selected by the Government as the best place to establish the works of British Dyes Limited, on account of shortage of dyes and colourings hitherto almost exclusively supplied by Germany. Many former beauty spots and walks were then closed to the public, lofty chimneys and structures being erected. 'In this utilitarian age, beauty must take a back seat,' explained the press.

Loving Thoughts of Dad.

We miss you, Daddy, ever so,
But you are out to fight the foe;
Oh, we would be brave soldiers, too,
And grow up, Daddy, just like you.
—MADE IN ST. CLAIR.

DURING THE FIRST WORLD WAR, Bamforths of Holmfirth caught the sentimental, tear-jerking mood of the time with their song cards. Local youngsters posed for cards like this. Gertrude and Walter Middleton are the older children. Gertrude later married butcher, Stanley Lewis. The verse on a similar card on which they featured is:

O God, please bless our Daddy brave,
Who's more than we can tell,
To Mam and us, – and keep him safe,
From every shot and shell;
And when he's won the great big war,
Please send him back, quite well.

A SOLDIER AND HIS NIECE. Henry O'Hara used to live in Turnbridge. Here he is with his niece Carrie. Harry, who had emigrated to Australia before the war, joined the Australian Commonwealth forces and went to France. On his way to England to visit Carrie he slipped off the gangplank, fell in between the ship and dock and drowned. One of the painful ironies of war. Henry never married. In March 1916 there were two zeppelin raid alarms in Huddersfield. Trams and vehicles had to remain stationary until 3 a.m. when 'all over' was given. The airships did not gain Huddersfield.

NURSES AND PATIENTS AT BRADLEY LANE TB AND WAR HOSPITAL. In 1911 a new specialized tuberculosis hospital, Bradley Wood Sanatorium, was conceived. Later it was used as a war hospital, and extended in 1935. The site of the sanatorium and a percentage of the buildings and equipment, namely the children's block and administration block, were the gift of Mr John Sykes JP of Acre House, Lindley, who died on 9 August 1914. On 4 October 1915 Royds Hall, at the top of Paddock, was opened by Mrs Joseph Blamires, Mayoress, as another hospital for wounded soldiers. Huddersfield was the only place in the country which provided a military hospital without any expense falling on the War Office. Subscriptions fell short of the total, but an anonymous donor with £300 covered the difference.

NURSE MABEL FRANCE, born at Kirkheaton on 27 June 1894, helped many of the war wounded at Bradley Gate hospital to recover both physically and mentally. Bryan Cooke, her son, recalls her happy personality, always singing the songs of the day. A special favourite of hers came from the musical *Our Miss Gibbs* – 'I feel so silly when the moon comes out – hopping, skipping – never, never stopping.' Mabel married Rowland Porteus Cooke, later living at 390 Prospect Terrace, Golcar. She married in 1926 aged thirty-five and considered her nursing days the happiest ones of her life. She died on 20 October 1952.

TIME FOR A CIGARETTE in a TB hospital! At that time some believed that smoking killed disease. Note the large old-fashioned deck chairs propped up against the wall by the standing soldier. Fingers trapped while endeavouring to put one of those into sitting position must have added to the already numerous injuries.

TWO SOLDIER PATIENTS, wearing medals, convalescing at Bradley Lane hospital. Lots of the young soldiers fell for the nurses. One Private Edginton gave Nurse France a watch. When she declined it, along with his attentions, he stamped on it smashing it to pieces in his anger. On 9 October 1915 the first train of wounded arrived in Huddersfield and most were sent to Royds Hall hospital. It was reported that on 24 December Christmas bells would not be rung in 1916. Turkey was scarce, and quite beyond the ordinary purse. Soldiers in local military hospitals, however, had a right royal time.

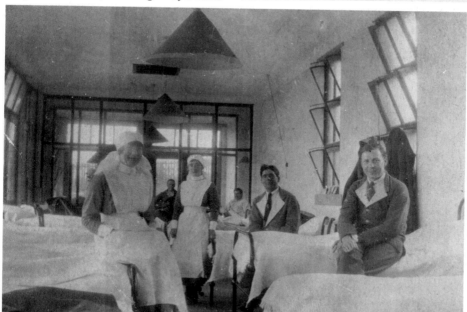

INSIDE ONE OF THE WARDS. Windows were left wide open to let in maximum fresh air and light. Nurse Mabel France is in the centre. Also on 9 October 1915, Madame Clara Butt's concert in the Town Hall gave part of the proceeds to war funds. In December that year a local dyers' dispute was settled by an increased war bonus.

A FEATURE OF TB HOSPITALS was beds being placed outside the building as much as possible. Here, one soldier looks as though he is trying to warm his hands beneath the sheets. On 11 December 1915 a Mrs Brown of Armitage Bridge, then aged 78, completed knitting 100 pairs of socks for soldiers at the front. They probably needed them at Bradley Gate too!

SISTER BAXTER ENJOYING A FEW QUIET MOMENTS seated on a fallen tree in Bradley wood. The weather must have been fine then, but June 1916 in Huddersfield was the coldest since 1909. That Whitsuntide was made a working holiday and children's Whitsun holidays were sacrificed to war munitions demands. However, on the Monday and Tuesday more than half the schoolchildren absented themselves and railway bookings were increased. Under Government auspices, a 12,000 ft film, *Britain Prepared*, was exhibited at the Town Hall.

GEORGE HAROLD BRUMMIT who suffered shell shock during the First World War. On 17 July 1916 a convoy of wounded soldiers, many direct from the 'big push' in France, came to Huddersfield. One of the wounded was one of the first patients sent to the Huddersfield Bradley Gate hospital.

A GROUP OF WOUNDED SOLDIERS posing outside the hospital at Bradley Gate. There appear to have been many smiling faces during those times of adversity. Could it have been those wonderful war songs such as 'Tipperary', 'Roses of Picardy' and 'Pack Up Your Troubles in Your Old Kit Bag' that kept their spirits high?

THERE WERE PLENTY OF AMUSEMENTS TO STAVE OFF BOREDOM while recovering in hospital. Both nurses and patients well enough to take part gave pierrot and other concerts at Bradley Gate. Nurse Mabel France is the central pierrot, seated, and it looks like Sister Baxter standing behind her. In July 1916 a fund was opened by the mayor with a donation of £15 for the formation of a Huddersfield War Concert Party to visit the front.

THE BRIDEGROOM on this First World War photograph was Harry Lees, in peacetime the 'local bobby' in Holmfirth. From left to right: Harry's sister, Bertha; Thomas Lees; the vicar; Sam Wood. Seated: W. Marshall, the groom, bride Annie Wood, the bridegroom's other sister Sarah Ann. Annie kept a General Store in Station Road, Holmfirth, opposite Bamforth's, photographers, after Harry was killed during the war. Her sister-in-law went to live with Annie to help her.

A WELL-KNOWN HUDDERSFIELD FACE, that of Maurice Addy, a cook during the war, later, working in 'civvy street' for Huddersfield Corporation tramways department. In the mills long hours weaving khaki, with poor gas-lighting, were soul destroying. Lads went round with a light on the end of a stick, and in the blackout some had to walk to the mill along the canal bank. They took a jam jar with a candle stuck inside, carrying it by a bit of string.

THOMAS QUARMBY, whose parents owned a quarry at Crosland Hill. The business commenced around the same time as Wimpenny's, the builders, before the First World War. In 1916 the Battle of Jutland claimed many, including the sixteen-year-old Thomas who was drowned there. At home that July a strike of Corporation gravediggers was in progress. Men were in receipt of 34s. and were demanding a war bonus of 2s.

A COUPLE OF HUDDERSFIELD 'MASHERS' (lady killers) portraying the lighter side of the First World War. The waxed moustache of the seated gentleman must have been something of a passion killer, though. Dandies and music hall songs typified the era. With Christmas in view, the 'Guardians' granted 1s. for each adult and 6d. for each chargeable child extra relief during the Christmas fortnight. These gentlemen, however, could obviously easily afford new gaiters, leggings, overshoes, boots and slippers — perhaps buying from Arthur Guest, 'The Bootman', 48 King Street.

WHEN ALFRED TAYLOR, son of grocer John Taylor, of Deighton, was brought home from Rugeley Camp for burial, the hearse bearing his coffin had to remain outside the house while a service was held. Having died with meningitis and 'spotted fever' it was not thought safe for the body to be brought inside. During the burial service another soldier was seen to be rolling about the graveyard with unsteady gait. Some thought him to be drunk, but he was suffering from shell shock.

SECTION THREE

Work

WILLIAM COUSINS, left, foreman jam maker at Wallace's with a colleague. William started work at the age of thirteen. He was born in 1870 and died in 1933. One of his tasks was to scrape wasps and spiders away from the top of jam then re-boil it. Wallace's, 'The People's Grocers', were down King Street and also had branches in other districts. Their Golden Flower Tea – 'Best Value in the Kingdom', – cost 1s. 8d., 2s., 2s. 4d. per lb in 1901. Shiny-backed black waistcoats covered with long white aprons also added to the charm of old-time Wallace's employees. Bletcher's jams, strawberry, raspberry, blackcurrant, made of choicest fruit and refined sugars were also enjoyed by Huddersfield people.

WILLIAM COUSINS, left, and a fellow worker, grinding coffee in Wallace's factory on St John's Road prior to the First World War. There did not seem to be the problems with food that we have these days. Could it be we do not adhere to the advice given in an almanack of that year: 'Eat only pure food, drink only pure liquids, think only pure thoughts, and keep your blood pure.'

A PORTRAIT OF WILLIAM COUSINS by Wm. Hirst, Close Hill, Lockwood. Cousins had a glass eye, he lost his own by vigorously pulling at a string while untying a parcel in childhood, with the help of a fork. For those injured in the factories, a Workman's Compensation Act came into operation on 1 July 1898. Although employers were liable for all accidents, even when caused by negligence, an employer was not liable under the Act for any injury which did not disable the workman for a period of at least two weeks from earning full wages at his work.

A PORTRAIT BY BAMFORTH'S OF HOLMFIRTH. Sarah Ann Lees, left, later Mrs McLoughlin of Bentley Street, Lockwood, with Annie Lees. Annie had a general store on Station Road, Holmfirth, and before Sarah was married she worked at the shop in exchange for board and lodging. When Sarah had three daughters they benefited by having lovely toys given from the Holmfirth shop, that their parents would not have been able to afford. Mrs McLoughlin died in 1976.

JOHN WOOD'S POULTRY, GAME AND FISH SHOP at the corner of Victoria Street in the 1930s. They used to employ a night watchman to stay in the shop all night as poultry could not all be taken down. The canvas blind seen running round the outside of the shop was rolled down after the shop closed. John Wood is on the left, Harold Holroyd standing with hands on hips, looks as though he is wearing clogs. During the Second World War queues used to form all the way round Victoria Lane and to the market. Henry Wood began the business in 1898 in Market Walk, moving in 1900 to the premises on the photograph. The same family continues the business, but in the new market hall. No more standing outside in winter weather. In 1970 the YEB was built where the old shop used to be.

MRS THORNTON, née Inman, of the mineral water manufacturers, photographed with a Bible on her knee. Note the old fashioned spectacles. One can imagine her reading the *Huddersfield Examiner*, costing only a halfpenny a copy at the beginning of the century. Seth Senior and Bentley and Shaw's were other mineral water manufacturers. In 1897 there was an advert for '"Zozo" — a sparkling, effervescing drink — £5 reward. See coupon in each tin. At all stores and grocers, 4d. Sole manufacturers, Rothery & Co. Huddersfield'.

JOHN TAYLOR, grocer, in the back garden behind the shop at Deighton. As can be seen, rhubarb was plentiful in his back garden. When John was serving a customer behind the counter one busy Saturday morning he suddenly disappeared from view. The old floorboards had given way beneath him! Joe, his son, rushed down into the cellar, expecting the worst. The old man was standing with a wry smile on his face, brushing bits of plaster from his head. 'It could have been worse' was his only comment.

TWO HUDDERSFIELD LADIES busy at a sewing machine. Harriet and Rose Sheard perhaps?. At the beginning of this century George Saville & Co., Wholesale and Retail Drapers, at 4 and 6 Queen Street, charged wholesale prices to Sewing Societies. Poor families often made children's clothing from best parts of adults' clothes. Others were clothed by Cinderella Society and similar charitable institutions. Most shops closed at 1 p.m. on Wednesdays, including W. Nicholson & Bros, 4 Kirkgate, who sold Combination Dresses in Scotch wool, Llama, and Merino. 'Shirts & Collars made to Measure, pyjama sleeping suits, cardigan jackets, gloves, scarves,and umbrellas sold.'

BROUGHTON COUSINS, an employee of Huddersfield Railway, in Kidroyd, at the end of Forest Road, Dalton, in 1920. He has a carbide lamp on his bicycle. Broughton lived at Aldmondbury Bank.

HERBERT TRUELOVE AND HIS DOG GIPSY, of the Old Toll House, Bradley Bar. A farm labourer and odd job man, Herbert was an outstandingly good artist. Once he was offered the chance to go to London to further a career as an artist, but he considered that a shallow type of life. He loved the countryside, and could paint life-like animals. Living through the Second World War years, when the first air raid siren shrilled in 1939 he was so upset he ran out into the garden and clambered inside the dustbin for shelter. He had neither cellar or air raid shelter. Being tall and thin, he couldn't accommodate his shoulders beneath the lid, and had violent cramp when eventually he emerged. Herbert always carried a ferret and caught hares for the farmer, who gave him one for himself at Christmas time.

FRANK WALKER, OF LEEDS ROAD, who used to work at John Lee Walker's mill. In leisure time Frank 'followed' the horses, and could give tips to racing fans that rarely failed to score. Frank had a good tip for bald men — always wear a hat, which he invariably did, indoors and out.

DINNER

in the Town Hall, Huddersfield, on
Friday, 28th May, 1926, at 6-30 p.m.

in recognition of the valuable services
rendered by the
VOLUNTEER BUSMEN & LOYAL TRAMWAYMEN.

Ald. T. CANBY, J.P.
Chairman, Tramways Committee.

THE DINNER MENU in the Town Hall, 28 May 1926, in recognition of the valuable services rendered by the volunteer busmen and loyal tramwaymen. Maurice Addy's menu is signed both back and front by guests, including mayor, Law Taylor.

MAURICE ADDY in the Tramways Lost Property Office in town. Umbrellas were the most frequently lost objects on public transport. Maurice was a tram conductor on the Outlane to Waterloo route during the Second World War. He lived at 969 Leeds Road, and cycled home after a late shift. Maurice recalled how, when the alarm woke him for early morning shift, he skated across the bedroom oilcloth to stop the clock wakening all the neighbours. His wife Doris polished that oilcloth until it shone like a mirror.

A GROUP OF FARNLEY TYAS WORKMEN.

COAL MINER SAM FRANCE of Upper Heaton. He worked in a 'Day Hole' in Bradley Wood during the First World War. When he was dying in 1917, a pedlar was outside in the street shouting 'oranges'. Sam's death was brought on by working in coal dust, and his last oranges, which his wife went to buy from the hawker in the street, soothed his last moments.

DEIGHTON COBBLER CHARLES SPENCER is seen here with his daughter Muriel feeding hens corn. His son Roy became a cobbler as well. Many wore clogs in those days, and hearing mill girls hurrying to work over the cobbled roads in them was a familiar sound. Another clogger, boot and shoe repairer was John Wm. Battye of 10 Hillhouse Road, off Bradford Road. Repairs were taken in at his residence, 11 Sheepridge Road.

TWO HUDDERSFIELD WEAVERS wearing black sateen type aprons, perhaps 1930s vintage. The deafening noise of looms made the art of lip reading almost essential if any conversation was to be enjoyed at work. These women worked at Woods Worsted mill. During the wars production in mills was primarily of khaki for the war effort. Many textile workers did not return to mill work after the war. The Labour government of 1945 promoted employment of refugee workers from Eastern Europe. They were guaranteed a wage three pounds above ordinary worker's wages. Many ceased to vote for Labour after this.

THE CHINN FAMILY owned taxi cabs in Huddersfield. Blanche (seated, right) taught at a Golcar school, and also at Deighton Sunday School, besides being a leader of the Christian Endeavour. When Ramsden's in Westgate closed on account of the ill health of Mr T.W. Chinn in 1931, Huddersfield lost its oldest café, which started in 1868. He also ran the last service of horse buses from Market Place to Birkby.

MEMBERS OF CLOTH HALL EXCHANGE. Included in the picture is Sam Suthers who was a wool buyer for Crowthers of Milnsbridge in the 1920s. All but the small boy are wearing bowler hats or trilbies. Cloth caps were for everyday wear and came into being as a result of mill owners wanting to use up ends of cloth. The sign behind the men reads John Eccles Limited Cotton Spinners, and Thomas Hudson. The Cloth Hall Exchange was pulled down to build the Ritz cinema. The Ritz cost £100,000 to build and was opened on 10 February 1936. Pride of place was given to a £10,000 Wurlitzer organ. The first film was a Walt Disney coloured 'Silly Symphony' followed by a stage performance of Billy Cotton and his Broadcasting Band, concluding with the musical film *First a Girl*, featuring Jessie Matthews. After the opening performance, guests were entertained to a cabaret show in the Ritz café. Organist Stanley Bishop gave his farewell performance, before conscription to HM Forces, in 1941.

EDGAR THORNTON AND FAMILY at their Northumberland Street home across from the old Prime Hotel. Edgar, greengrocer, had twelve barrow boys working for him all over Huddersfield and district. His wife Clara was a worker for Queen Street Mission, and bought every unmarried mother a first set of baby clothes. Clara's parents had a dairy on Northgate, before the First World War. Clarence, centre front, died aged nineteen. Edgar's sister Kate had a high class millinery shop on Wood Street.

SOME OF THE STAFF OF HENRY BOOTH'S WHOLESALE CLOTHIERS, Viaduct Street. It was burnt down on 31 October 1941. Many girl workers were killed during the fire, by jumping out to try and save their lives. A policeman had the misfortune to see his own daughter jump out. This photo includes Reggie Priestley (fourth right), Mr and Mrs Slater and Wilfred Booth.

EMPLOYEES OF KARRIER WORKS on Deadwaters, Longroyd Bridge. John George McLoughlin, coach painter and sign writer, is standing eighth from the right on the back row (braces showing). He was in the Home Guard during the Second World War and lived at Bentley Street, Lockwood.

ALL WORK AND NO PLAY? How the working man used to enjoy his works outing – and still does. John George McLoughlin, front centre, 'slakes' his thirst.

PETER AND BETTY WHITMARSH, fish and chip shop owners on Leeds Road in the 1930s, with their children. A 'fish and pennorth' was a favourite quick meal, eaten from the newspaper. Betty seems to be wearing a then fashionable 'edge-to-edge' coat.

JOE DICKINSON, left, walking in town with Kenneth Sykes. In later years Joe was a night watchman, always with his pipe for company. Joe had been a joiner. Kenneth, who lived on Town Avenue, Leeds Road, used to sell newspapers.

MABEL COOKE (she used to be Nurse France) with husband Rowland Porteus, and son Bryan, at 390 Prospect Terrace, Scar Lane, Golcar in 1931. Rowland was gardener for sixteen years at Ashfield, Station Road, Golcar. How typical of the thirties is Mabel's print overall, and hair simply parted at one side and held back by a kirby grip. Like most men of the time, Rowland has the inevitable cigarette. Bryan was only fifteen when his mother died.

HARRY BARROWCLOUGH, gardener at Oaklands Home for the Elderly, tends flowers in the grounds at Dalton, Greenhead Lane, in the 1960s. At Christmas Harry used to make splendid decorations for the old ladies resident there. Now they have all gone, the windows are boarded up and huge, friendly Bruno, the labrador, who loved to loll on the lawn in summer and keep the ladies company, is only a memory. The house was originally owned by the Tolson family.

TITANIC MILL, LINTHWAITE, built in 1912. It was nicknamed Titanic after the ship went down in April that year. Otherwise it was known as the Colne Valley Spinning Company. Harriet Wood used to go there in 1926 to help her dad polish the machinery. Mr Wood was a boiler firer.

BRYAN COOKE, RIGHT, WITH FRED BOOTLAND AND HIS WIFE EDITH. Fred used to work at Blamires mill. Edith, when Miss Truelove, also worked in a mill. Bryan was employed in the Estate Offices.

ROBERT LODGE WAS A BROKER, living at Whitehead Lane, Primrose Hill, in the early years of the century. He regularly visited Southport sales, writing postcards home instructing his wife that a sideboard or other item would be arriving at Huddersfield station at a certain time, and someone must be there to meet the train with the wagon. One postcard he wrote in pencil on 18 December 1904, reads 'We have had a lovely day here, just like summer'. So it isn't only nowadays that the weather sometimes goes haywire!

ARTHUR FIRTH AND HIS WIFE of Gipsy Lane (now known as Greenhead Lane), Dalton. Hawking fish was Arthur's trade, but every Friday night he went to Moldgreen Liberal Club and bought everybody a pork pie. Thus nicknames are born. Thereafter he was generally known as 'Pie' Firth. Norman Hopkinson was another who used to go around houses selling his wares. His trade was pots, pans and china. Gaily decorated chamberpots swayed from hooks round his wagon.

LONG-DISTANCE LORRY DRIVER ALBERT BAILEY in the late twenties or thirties. Employed by Hanson's, he drove through the night to London sometimes three times a week. In leisure moments he enjoyed playing billiards and 'having a gill'. Albert and his wife Harriet lived at Linthwaite.

A GROUP OF HUDDERSFIELD LADIES on an outing to Dickinson's Longley farm in the 1960s. Edgar and Joseph Dickinson, sons of a local farmer, expanded their dairy at Holmfirth until their products became a household name. The Dickinson doctrine is 'Supply real dairy produce, fresh products of top quality, at a competitive price'.

WHEN THE MONEY HAS BEEN EARNED, there have to be banks to save it in! Roger Smith, left, worked for the Midland Bank before joining the Royal Air Force in the 1940s. Philip Taylor, centre, was at King Street National Provincial Bank, with here, right, school friend, Leslie Moorhouse. Roger now lives in Haywards Heath, Leslie and his wife Wyn have left Huddersfield for the sunnier, warmer climes of Torquay. Philip died in 1978.

DAVID BROWN GEAR WORKS, LOCKWOOD, another employer of many Huddersfield people. Here are some of the despatch office on 3 June 1950. Front left to right: Bill Barras, Hazel Taylor (in hat), Barbara Mitchell, Leslie Sykes, all seated. Hilton Bamforth leans against the wall on the right. Raymond Castle and Luther Dyson also worked in despatch. Mavis Wise left Brown's that spring to work as a dental receptionist for £4 3s. 6d. per week. On 5 October I had a 5s. pay rise, bringing my gross wage up to the majestic sum of £4. This was celebrated with lunch in Collinson's café, feeling rich. When working on a Saturday we dressed up — even wearing a hat — for shopping in town afterwards.

ICI EMPLOY MANY HUDDERSFIELD PEOPLE. Two former employees, Ruth and Audrey North, pose on a wall with a friend in the war years. Ruth later worked at the Gas Board, living at Aldmondbury Bank. She died in 1989. Audrey lives in Harrogate. The sisters lived at Longhill Road, Sheepridge.

ANOTHER COUPLE OF EX-ICI EMPLOYEES. Pictured outside Bradley Gate Sanatorium Lodge in 1946, Edith McLoughlin, left, and Irene Taylor with canine friend. Mr and Mrs Taylor were then living at the Lodge as caretakers. Irene is now, unfortunately, in a hospital in York. Edith married Philip Walker and lives at Salendine Nook. Treats after work included tea in the Kingsway café down King Street, Fox's dancing class, re-unions with boys who were being demobbed from the services, or simply listening to the wireless.

WILLIAM COUSINS, in working clothes — or were they his Sunday best? Around this period Edgar Lord, Upholsterer and House Furnisher, was at 26 Buxton Road. William Calverley & Co., shirt and collar makers, John William Street and St Peter Street, sold gentlemen's collars at 2s. 3d. for half a dozen. Sykes's Embrocation was available at 4 Packhorse Yard and Moldgreen, and was recommended for rubbing on the chest in bronchitis and whooping cough. One shilling per bottle. There would be no side-effects with that!

A WOMAN'S WORK IS NEVER DONE. Annie Crowther, Whitehead Lane, Primrose Hill, nursing Kathleen in 1909. W. Thomas at 59 New Street, Huddersfield, general and fancy draper, sold baby linen and infants' layettes. 'Also corset specialists — "Ask for the new Platinum corset".' Childhood was a time for medicines — Sykes' Autumn and Spring Medicine for the blood and skin cost $7\frac{1}{2}$d. and 1s. a bottle, and who can forget the horror of California Syrup of Figs, and Fennings Fever Cure? Cod Liver Oil emulsion, however, was flavoured so as to remove the taste of oil. 1s. and 1s. 8d. per bottle.

Chapels, Churches and Sunday Schools

THERE WAS NO NEED TO SEEK ELSEWHERE FOR SOCIAL LIFE when chapel or church was the focal point of village life! Mill, shop, and factory workers were transformed into Gilbert and Sullivan characters when they took part in operettas. Performers in Deighton Methodist *HMS Pinafore* in the early thirties include Joe Taylor, centre front, boater hat, Henry Dryer, far right. A bit of a furore arose over certain incidents. Someone said 'dammit' in the libretto, and Mr Passant and other chapel leaders objected. Mr Priestley, choir master, was written to and future scores had first to be submitted to them. Muriel Cheetham, facing right, extending a graceful hand, stands to the right of Joe.

ANOTHER SCENE FROM *HMS PINAFORE*. The more extrovert members of the chapel are taking part, including: Joe Taylor, on the bridge with Annie Crawshaw; Nellie Armitage; Mary Walton and Hilda Gibson. Marjorie Crawshaw and Mildred Dyson are on the steps. Wright Charlesworth and Tom Jessop are to their left. Muriel Cheetham is standing fifth from the right. Blanche Chinn is on the centre of the back row. Choir master Arthur Nunn Priestley is far left on the front row. Also included are: Donald Oddy; Olive Crawshaw; Dorothy Priestley, next to man with patch over eye; Reggie Priestley, the small boy in front; Allen Dyson far right.

HMS PINAFORE. On the bridge, Donald Oddy and young Reggie Priestley. Far left is Frank Wadsworth. On the right, bending, is Stanley Dawson as Dick Dead Eye. Others in the 'Sailors Chorus' are Ben Pearson, John Howarth, Jack Bland, Harold Charlesworth, Stanley Dawson, and Joe Taylor in the centre, with hands on hips.

HER LADYSHIP performed at Deighton. Vera Whitehead, centre, pictured in the mirror, had the title role. Winifred Holmes holds the mirror for her. Also pictured are Dorothy Walker, Madge Brook, Vera Knapton and Marion Ainley.

DEIGHTON MARRIED LADIES CONCERT, coached by Mrs Cheetham, seated far right, middle row. Oh, the gusto that was put into the singing and marching of 'There's Something About a Soldier!' On the front row, seated is Mrs Alice Bailey. The choir master's wife Ada Priestley is second from the right, daughter Mabel is on the far right. Hilda Taylor is the tall 'soldier' far right. Other well-known faces of the time were Mrs Matt (Martha) Varley, Mrs Agnes Pratt, Mrs Woodworth, Mrs Raynor and Mrs Sally Charlesworth.

MARY PEARSON, centre, was secretary of Deighton Chapel and a choir member for years. Joe Taylor, acting with her, frequently supplied provisions for events from his shop. Dorothy Priestley, in riding breeches, gazes up at Donald Oddy, right. Joe embarrassed Mary in the final act when he sent out, unbeknown to her, for a couple of packets of fish and chips and presented one to her on the bridge.

THE NEW AND RETIRING DEIGHTON SUNDAY SCHOOL QUEENS posing with attendants in the graveyard in the 1930s. Joyce Walker is third from the left with a cloak and holding a bouquet. Jean Woodworth is third right. Villager Mrs Howarth looks over the wall. The Dutch bonnets worn by the attendants were fashionable. Glenfield Avenue is the row of houses in the background.

A SCENE FROM ONE OF THOSE LOVELY MARRIED LADIES CONCERTS of the early thirties, again at Deighton. Hilda Taylor, centre, dressed as a gentleman in mauve satin, white stockings, and wig for 'When I Grow Too Old To Dream' with Ada Priestley, the choir master's wife. The ladies who were better at sewing than singing made the costumes – the dresses were composed entirely of pink crepe paper. Hilda used to take a bottle of port and packet of mint imperials to hand round to the cast prior to the big event of 'First Night'. What fun they had. Especially at one performance when Mrs Fred Wood, the fish and chip shop owner's wife, spied a mouse scurrying across the stage and leapt on to a table.

:: DEIGHTON ::
METHODIST SUNDAY SCHOOL.

Programme for
Whit-Monday, 5th June, 1933,
INCLUDING THE
Crowning of the
Sunday School Queen Elect.
(MISS JOYCE WALKER)

1-30 p.m. Procession of Teachers and Scholars leaves Sunday School, headed by the Retiring Sunday School Queen (Miss Winifred Holmes) and Retinue.

1-35 p.m. Sing at top of Whitacre Street.

The Procession will proceed to the War Memorial, on which a Wreath will be placed by the Sunday School Queen.

The Procession then proceeds to Sunny View, for a United Sing with the Teachers and Scholars of the Sheepridge Providence Methodist, Sheepridge Wiggan Lane Methodist, and Woodhouse Church of England Sunday Schools at 2-15 p.m.

The Procession, including the Queen and Retinue, will then proceed to Bradley Wood Sanatorium.

4-0 p.m. A Public Tea will be served in the Sunday School at a charge of 6d.

Crowning Ceremony in the Church.

Friends are requested to assemble in the Church not later than 6 p.m. After the Ceremony, the friends are invited to join the Teachers and Scholars in the field on North Sides, kindly lent for the occasion by Mr. F. Gawthorp.

All old Scholars and Parents of present Scholars are very cordially invited to take part in the Procession.

ANOTHER YEAR, ANOTHER SUNDAY SCHOOL QUEEN. The pattern of Sunday School life was the same, year after year, up to the Second World War. Public teas were a feature of anniversaries and similar occasions. The leaders meetings made arrangements as to who would cater, and what would be served. For seventy it was suggested $\frac{1}{2}$ stone plain loaves, a dozen mixed teacakes, 6 brown loaves, 4 sandwiches, 6 dozen buns, 4 currant loaves, 2 lb hardcakes, 4 moulds potted beef. Jam, butter, tea, milk, etc. as necessary. In the minutes book someone pencilled in later 'a lot left over'. Lady members of the leaders were usually asked to prepare the tea, and some served as tray holders. Leftovers would probably be attended to by the Poor Steward, Mr Donald Oddy.

THERE WAS BRILLIANTLY SUNNY WEATHER for the Deighton United Methodist Sunday School May queen celebration on Whit Monday, 16 May 1932. The retiring queen, Miss Rosie Gannon, and her retinue left the Sunday School and proceeded to the war memorial. The Revd A.H. Sharman led the gathering in prayer. After the service, the procession proceeded to Sunny View for a united 'sing' with teachers and scholars of Sheepridge Providence and Wesleyan Sunday Schools, and then went on to Bradley Gate Sanatorium. Attendants' white dresses were 'run up' by a local dressmaker if the mother was not capable of sewing them.

SUNDAY SCHOOL QUEEN, ROSIE GANNON, and a motor car at the top of Whitacre Street. Days were not always to prove as bright for Rosie – her husband was drowned during the Second World War. From October 1940 until lighter weather, morning and afternoon services only were held in chapel, due to the blackout.

SUNDAY SCHOOL QUEEN ROSIE GANNON and retinue in procession up Deighton Road, 1932. In the evening chapel was crowded for the crowning of the new queen, Miss Winifred Holmes. Mr David Crawshaw, chairman, appealed to parents to send children to Sunday School. The crowning of the queen was performed by Mrs Blamires, who pronounced her 'a right regular royal Queen'. Mrs Blamires suggested that perhaps a Sunday School king might be appointed next year from among the boys. When Rosie, the 'dethroned queen' rose to respond to the expression of appreciation of past services by Miss M. Pearson, she was quite overcome, but after a brief respite she delivered a 'splendid little address'.

DEIGHTON CHAPEL has now been demolished. Mr E.A. Leatham, MP for Huddersfield, laid the foundation stone on 27 November 1875. The cost was estimated at £3,300. Further burial ground accommodation was given behind the Sunday School in 1919, due to the efforts of Mr W.D. Poppleton. During the First World War, when organist Mr Priestley was away on military service, duties were shared by Miss Anna Poppleton and Miss Doris B. Medley.

DEIGHTON CHAPEL.

Deighton Methodist Church.

Thanksgiving Day,

Saturday, December 3rd, 1932.

3-0 to 7 p.m.   The Minister will sit in the Church Vestry to receive your Thankoffering.

4-30 p.m.   TEA in the Schoolroom.   ::   Adults 8d. Children 6d.

6-30 to 7 p.m.   Community Hymn-Singing in the Church. Led by Mr. D. E. Varley.

7-0 p.m.   **GREAT THANKSGIVING MEETING** in the Church.

WILLIAM SHIRES, Esq., J.P. will preside.

Speaker :

Rev. LEONARD HALEY, M.A. (Highfield Congregational Church).

Supported by Rev. John Burton, Superintendent Minister, and Rev. J. T. Passant, Minister, and Sunday School Queen (Miss Winifred Holmes).

The Children will present their offerings to the Sunday School Queen at the Evening Meeting.

Apart from this, no collection will be taken.

Special Music by the Choir under the direction of Mr. Priestley.

SPECIAL DAYS kept interest alive in church activities. In the thirties, one-act plays by F.A. Carter were popular, as were home produce sales. At one of these, former choirmaster D. Ellis Varley recalled the days when there was a 'striker-up' to start the singing in churches.

FRED LANGLEY, ASSISTANT SECRETARY OF DEIGHTON CHAPEL, lived at Kirkburton in North Road in 1940. The photograph was by Thomas Dent. Being of caustic wit, one Sunday, when young scholar, Dorothy Priestley, arrived late for Sunday School, Fred bawled out, much to her dismay, 'Oh Dorothy, if I get to know of a house nearer Sunday School, I'll let you know.'

DEIGHTON CHAPEL MEMBERS all set for an outing. Included are: Maurice Addy, Mary Pearson, Nellie Gibson, Mrs Lockwood (chapel caretaker), Mrs Sutton, Mr and Mrs Harry Medley. Chapel caretaker Mr Lockwood is in the front seat of the bus. These excursions, to Lake Windermere or other beauty spots, did not have the usual alcohol content that typifies some get-togethers. But it did have plenty of good companions, good cheer, and excellent singing!

MISS ADA TRUELOVE, pictured in the 1930s. Ada lived at Bradley Lane Toll Bar House with her father, Herbert, and sister Edith. As with many, money was scarce. Ada and Edith were great friends with Hilda Taylor who lived at the shop they called at on their way home from the mill. Hilda used to parcel up some of her outfits for the girls. Eagerly, they would have a peep as they walked up the old 'Shockey' lane on their way home. This is one of the outfits Ada liked, including the then-fashionable fur-backed gauntlet gloves.

A WET DAY OUT IN THE EARLY THIRTIES or late twenties for Nellie Gibson, standing, far left, Hilda Taylor, Hilda Gibson, Joe Taylor in bowler hat, Philip Taylor and Marjorie Crawshaw at the front. A bit of rain did not worry members of Deighton Chapel Choir. They could always 'Sing as We Go, and Let the World Go By'.

DEIGHTON METHODIST CHURCH.

On Wednesday, January 17th, 1934,

at 7-30 p.m., in the Schoolroom,

: A :

SUBSCRIPTION CONCERT

will be given by

The "Huddersfield" Male Voice Quartet.

FORMED OCTOBER 31ST. 1931.

E. ARMITAGE.	H. COUPLAND.	T. A. CREASER.	G. E. JESSOP.
1ST TENOR.	2ND TENOR.	BARITONE	BASS.

COMPETITIVE SUCCESSES - 1933

First Prize,   Morecambe Musical Festival, May, 1933.
Second Prize,   Wallasey Musical Festival, October, 1933.
First Prize and Shield,   Leicester Musical Festival, October, 1933.
Silver Bowl for best of Male and Mixed Classes. From a list of 30 Quartets, Leicester Musical Festival, October, 1933

This makes a total of 13 First Prizes and 1 Second Prize out of 14 entries for Contests.

With Humorous and Musical Interludes by Mr. NORMAN FULLER and Madame DORIS HAIGH.

TICKETS - 2/- & 1/-

CHILDREN UNDER 14 HALF-PRICE.

The entire proceeds of this effort will be used to purchase a supply of the New Methodist Hymn Book for use in the Church Services—estimated cost £30. The expenses of this Concert are being met by private gifts, which means that every ticket bought will be a direct subscription towards the purchase of a Hymn Book costing 2/3 each. Will YOU help, please ?

Tickets obtainable at the Shops of Miss Crawshaw and Mr. John Taylor.

T. WOFFENDEN, BIRKBY.

ONLY TWO SHILLINGS OR A SHILLING, children under fourteen half price, to listen to the Huddersfield Male Voice Quartet on 17 January 1934. Proceeds were to go to buy new hymn books which then cost 2s. 3d. each. In those days it was an honour to become a chapel member, and those wishing to do so were 'on trial' for a period prior to being accepted.

ANOTHER HAPPY OPERETTA AT DEIGHTON. Back row, left to right: Harry Medley, Jack Whitehead, Henry Dryer. Ladies: Marion Ainley, Mary Walton, Annie Crawshaw, Nellie Armitage, Mildred Dyson, Dorothy Walker, Lily Armitage, Winifred Holmes, Mary Dyson, Eileen Oddy, Madge Brook, Muriel Cheetham. Hilda Taylor is to the left behind the 'footman'. Her husband Joe is seated at the front, far left wearing a wig. Dorothy Priestley has Stanley Dawson's arm round her. Vera Whitehead, Donald Oddy, Fred Bailey, Louie Haggis, Frank Wadsworth are also included on the front row.

A VERY EARLY DEIGHTON METHODIST CONCERT PARTY. Deighton was the oldest Methodist chapel in Huddersfield. Janet Robinson, kneeling, front row, second right, married the Revd John Whyte.

HILDA AND JOE TAYLOR, in Sunday Best in the 1920s. Visiting ministers to the chapel were often entertained to dinner and tea at the couple's shop, 'Central Stores'. Cutlery was shined in a special machine beforehand, the Yorkshire Range in the back room polished brightly with blacklead. Beef, Yorkshire pudding, vegetables, followed by a huge rice pudding was the usual dinnertime fare.

ANOTHER GLORIOUS SOUND the modern generation rarely hears; that of a chapel or church organ playing sacred music. Here, Jimmy Ainley plays in Deighton chapel for the last wedding ever to be solemnized there, perhaps in 1958.

ST MARK'S CHURCH, LONGWOOD. In 1749 a chapel was erected at Longwood by private subscription, known as the Chapel of St Mark the Evangelist. A sundial on the south wall of the present church was made by Joseph Millar, master of the Free School. A bell for the chapel was cast in 1750, engraved 'Fear God, Honour the King'. The foundation stone of a new parish church was laid in August 1876 by W. Spencer Stanhope Esq. MP. On 29 October 1915 a sale of work was organized as the church at Longwood was about £500 in debt. The Bishop of Leeds, then the Revd Dr Cowgill, opened a new Catholic church at Longwood on 29 May 1917. Longwood Aid Society's demonstration and Gala, on 21 July 1917, realized over £600.

WOODHOUSE CHURCH, a pretty snow scene from days when gas lamps flickered to life when the lamplighter went on his rounds. In the church magazine of 1901, concern about the organ was expressed. Messrs Conacher, organ builders of Huddersfield, estimated that a new one would cost about £550. It could not be left as it was, it might break down any Sunday.

THE CHANCEL, ALDMONDBURY PARISH CHURCH. The Revd Charles Augustus Hulbert MA was vicar of Aldmondbury from 1867 until his death in 1888. He wrote the *Annals of the Church and Parish of Aldmondbury*. We learn that the parish was almost exclusively agricultural, and tythes of hay, lambs, wool, fowls, geese, doves, eggs, bees, honey, wax, flax, hemp, wood, trees and other obligations anciently and by right were due and customary to the Rector.

THE DEACONS, OF PRIMROSE HILL BAPTIST CHURCH, during the Second World War. Standing, from left to right: Jack Howard, Dorothy Atha, Arthur Howard, J.A. Goddard, Violet Pheasey. Front row: Norman Day (one time mayor), Margaret Blamires, Fred Woodhead, L. Waddington and Elsie Barker.

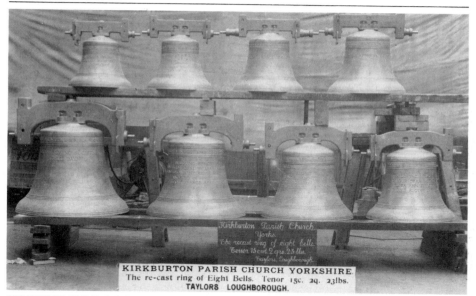

KIRKBURTON PARISH CHURCH YORKSHIRE.
The re-cast ring of Eight Bells. Tenor 15c. 2q. 23lbs.
TAYLORS LOUGHBOROUGH.

IMMEDIATELY ABOVE AND ON THE SOUTH SIDE OF THE FONT is an oak plaque with the inscription 'This peal of eight bells was recast by Taylor and Sons, Loughborough, on August 25th, 1919, and rung for the first time on Feb. 14th 1920. Dedicated January 9th, 1921, F.H. Sangster.' The bells were last fitted in 1987.

ST PATRICK'S CHURCH was solemnly opened on Wednesday 26 September 1932. The collection amounted to £130, a number of influential businessmen and mill owners contributed, though not of the Roman Catholic faith. One reason was the necessity of Irish labour, and many workers would not remain unless a place of worship was provided.

KIRKHEATON BELL RINGERS. Mr Senior, Mr Sykes, and Mr Bill Hargreaves, probably in the 1960s. Crosland Moor used to provide expert teams for this once popular pastime. The first, formed in 1890, connected with the Methodist Church, had the word 'United' added to the title of Crosland Moor Handbell Ringers when a dispute in 1905 resulted in the junior team breaking away to form the Crosland Moor Public Handbell Ringers. The United team won the National Championship First Prize in 1905/6/7 and 1910 and the Public team in 1901/2/3/9. The United team disbanded in 1911.

MORE KIRKHEATON BELL RINGERS. Crosland Moor Public team toured New Zealand in 1912 before disbanding in 1934.

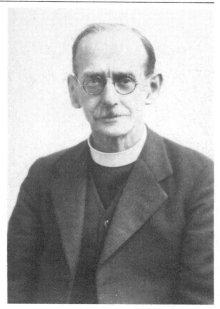

A PHOTOGRAPH OF THE REVD JOSEPH OGDEN, taken by Greaves of 55 New Street, Huddersfield. On the agenda at Deighton Methodist leaders meeting of 27 September 1933 was 'what shall we offer Mr Ogden for his services as lecturer at the Chapel Anniversary?' A gift of £1 was decided upon. However, in 1929 a Mr J. Hogg was only paid 10s. for his services, officiating all day at a flower service. Those who had a car were asked to offer transport to visiting ministers. The Revd Ogden's sermon was the 'Lighter Side of Life' (60 tales in 60 minutes).

LORNA DENNIS, CHRISTINE OLDROYD AND SUSAN LODGE, followed by Mr and Mrs Mellor, after a Christmas morning service at Dalton St Paul's in the 1960s. This chapel was destroyed by fire, but fortunately, unlike the fate of so many other local ones, another has been rebuilt in its place.

SLAITHWAITE PARISH CHURCH. The patron saint of the church was St James, and once a year what was originally intended as a fast became converted – or perverted – into a feast, to do honour to the name of the apostle. In the 1860s this was an annual holiday of three or four days given up to eating and drinking quantities of roast beef and home-brewed beer accompanied by pickled cabbage and plum pudding. If friends and neighbours elected to spend their time at the seaside they were dubbed as snobbish and disloyal to old customs, and called upon to answer the question, 'What was to come of 'Sanjimis' if we all went off and left it?'

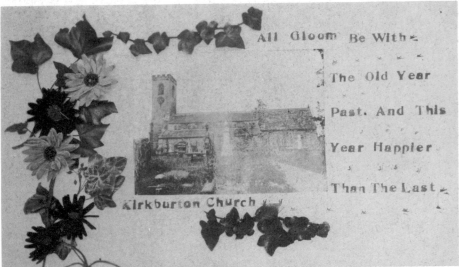

IN YEARS GONE BY there was a fashion for local churches to be incorporated on Christmas greetings cards. There is hope for better days in the verse. Kirkburton church was erected about the same time as those of Aldmondbury and Huddersfield. During the building of a portion of the chancel a broken crucifix was found built in the rubble of the east and north walls, dating back to the fourth century.

SECTION FIVE

Sport

PRIMROSE HILL BAPTIST CHURCH GYM CLASS in the early 1900s. Far left, standing, Herbert Atha, secretary. He later worked at Thomas Broadbent, Queen Street South, as foreman of maintenance and joinery. Far right, John William Atha, president of the club and owner of Watkinson & Co., engineering shop, Chapel Hill. Emerson Bros, 11 Market Street was one of the shops to go to for sports equipment. In 1935 tennis rackets cost between 18s. 6d. and 67s. 6d. Some chapels had tennis clubs.

JOE DICKINSON, who lost an arm in an accident at a printing works. Nevertheless, he was one of the best billiard players at Bradley Mills Working Men's Club. Joe Davis was a great idol of billiard fans and snooker players in the 1930s and '40s.

FAMILY GROUP of Joe Dickinson, wife and daughter. They lived at Town Crescent, Leeds Road. After losing an arm Joe was fitted with a hook.

SUMMERTIME IN THE THIRTIES, and time to emulate Len Hutton, George Herbert Hirst and Leary Constantine. Philip Taylor is in the back garden of Central Stores, Deighton. There used to be a grocers' cricket team who played at a ground in Lepton on Wednesday half-day closing. Once George Herbert Hirst was at Lepton, and I chased after him with my autograph book. The great man asked me to walk with him across the pitch; if he stopped to sign he would have a crowd round him. How proud I felt to actually be walking with him, knowing dad was watching in the crowd.

IDRIS TOWILL of Bridgend came to Huddersfield to play for the rugby league team in 1929 or '30. He and his wife Dilys lived at Bleasdale Avenue, Birkby. Idris captained Keighley when they won the cup at Wembly. He returned to Bridgend in 1940 and died — queuing to go into a match — on 21 september 1988, aged 78. Idris had worked for Huddersfield Electricity. Prior to the war he and Dilys danced at St Cuthbert's most Saturday evenings.

FARTOWN FOOTBALL FIELD. By the length of the boys shorts this must have been photographed in the 1920s or '30s. Rugby Union in Huddersfield dates back to 1866 when a rugby football section of the Huddersfield Athletic Club was formed. A meeting for the formation of a new club was called at the Pack Horse Hotel in 1909, and the Old Boys were created, a title that was to remain in Huddersfield Rugby Union football until after the Second World War when the club became plain Huddersfield.

A BODY-BUILDING GROUP at Milnsbridge. On the back row, second right is Sam Suthers.

JOE TAYLOR, GROCER, OF DEIGHTON, wins the coveted billiard cup and makes the moment immortal by posing with it – and a cigarette – on a deck chair in the back garden, probably in the late thirties. It would have been almost unheard of to miss a football match on Saturday afternoon. Wives and girlfriends went shopping, and a slap up tea was prepared for the supporters return. How the rest of the evening went depended upon who had won. Part of the time was usually spent at the local Liberal, Conservative, or working men's club playing billiards.

ANOTHER LOCAL AMATEUR FOOTBALL TEAM. Sydney Gregory is on the left, standing. He lived at Lockwood, then Cowlersley after his marriage. This was in the late twenties or early thirties. Rugby football has always been played in Huddersfield. A revived side, known as the Old Boys, were playing against the 'old Black Watch' at Kirkburton in about 1909. When Willie Ainley had his shirt torn off, the landlady from the 'local' sent along a starched shirt to replace it.

FRED LUNN PLAYING GOLF. Once a Town footballer and, later, landlord of the White Horse on Leeds Road. In Huddersfield at one time golf was regarded as a rich man's sport. Yet Fred would often run like the devil to the next fare stage on Leeds Road to save a halfpenny tram fare. Keenly interested in all sport was Dr Copland, who had a private practice in New North Road. He was a member of Outlane and Huddersfield Golf Clubs, and past president of Huddersfield Curling Club. He came to Huddersfield in 1911, and died in 1946.

ELLA LUNN, one time landlady of the White Horse, Leeds Road, enjoying a game on one of the Huddersfield courses. When she and Fred retired, they lived at Longley Road, Aldmondbury then Outlane, finally at Bare, Morecambe, playing golf as often as possible. Fixby Hall, used as a golf club today, was the former home of Richard Oastler, pioneer in the reform of factory conditions.

SECTION SIX

Leisure

A LEISURELY DRIVE THROUGH BEAUMONT PARK IN A LANDAU. Tom Turner is with his wife and baby Dorothy. Walking was still the chief leisure pursuit, however. Not surprising when one considers the disasters that could overtake when relying on public transport: On 5 May 1916 an Outlane tram car, returning to town, pulled up at West Hill when the pawl holding the hand brake slipped. The handle whirled round with such force that it knocked Wilson, the driver, down. The tram dashed away down the hill, but two passengers emerged from the lower saloon and applied the brakes in time to avert a disaster. Their service was afterwards recognized by the Corporation.

FOUR SISTERS in the latter years of the nineteenth century enjoy a pleasant summer day. The venue was probably Windyridge, Chestnut Street, Sheepridge. Standing, right, Janet Robinson, left, Clara, later Mrs Brook of Windyridge. In front, reading and knitting, Eliza and Fanny Robinson. Fancy wearing high-laced boots like those, when warm enough to sit outside! Clara, born 1866, worked for her husband John Robinson at the mill. She kept a policeman's helmet on top of a big cupboard in her home in case a burglar came — she thought it would scare him off.

SAM FRANCE IN BOWLER HAT enjoying a family get-together. Daughter Mabel, seated, far right, was born in 1892 and became a nurse at Bradley Gate Sanatorium. Her son Bryan still has a ringlet of hers — 'like spun gold'. Doris, seated far left, became Mrs Maurice Addy. The grate Sam stands on led into the cellar. Perishable goods were kept in basements. In hot weather milk was often thrown away or scones made from it after it had turned sour. The photograph was taken around 1902.

IN APRIL 1913 BAMFORTH'S of Holmfirth recommenced making films on a large scale. Nearly fifty comedies were completed before war stopped production in 1915.

BAMFORTH'S LITTLE DOG, NIPPER, who resembled the dog on 'His Master's Voice' records, was much in demand for sentimental song cards. The halfpenny green stamp on the back of the postcard is dated 20 August 1908. Mr Settle, Mrs Booth and Mary Johnson, who worked for Bamforth's, are also on the postcard. How long ago it seems, when the focal point of a room was the fireplace, and not the television set.

FANCY DRESS PARADES AND CHAPEL CONCERTS were among the main leisure pursuits in the twenties. Here, Janet Whyte is all dressed up for a concert in 1923. Janet and Fanny, her sister, made a pact that they would always say they were ten years younger than they were. Who said *men* were deceivers ever?

MISS ADA L. WARD LLA of Lindley, well known in the Huddersfield district for her poetry readings in the early years of the century. Monologues were also popular, and later on many tried to copy those such as 'The Lion and Albert' – not Miss Ward's type one would imagine. Ada was a friend of Annie Crowther, of Primrose Hill.

A CARNIVAL AT THE TOP OF BARGATE, Linthwaite. 'Comic Jim', as he was known, and Freddy Whittam were among the revellers, plus the inevitable brass band. Possibly a Whitsuntide procession in the 1930s. In 1935 Kahns in Huddersfield sold flannel trousers from 5s. 11d., sports jackets from 10s. 11d. And for crashing down on to when all that marching was over, Rushworths in town had garden chairs at 10s. 6d., single deck chairs 5s. 6d. and, if you were *really* extravagant, a couch hammock from £3 19s. 6d.

ANOTHER LINTHWAITE PROCESSION, possibly the same occasion. What handsome young men! The one at the side of the lorry resembles matinée idol, Ramon Novarro, who was starring with Evelyn Laye in *The Night is Young* on Saturday 22 June 1935 at the Tudor Cinema, Huddersfield.

JACK THE DOG, on his mat, fronting a family group at Nab Hill, Dalton. Councillor George Brown, far right, next to Nellie Brown, who died when aged only thirty-three. Grandma Brown is seated far right, with little Mabel Priestley in front. Arthur Haigh, at the back of the group, worked in the pattern room at Learoyds mill on Leeds Road. After tea visitors usually had a 'sing song' around the piano. Pianos could be bought from £16 10s. in 1903. Other popular instruments were concertinas, melodians, and Fairy Bells. Christmas carols on sheet music cost 3d. each from Biltcliffe Bros, Bridge Street, Penistone.

GOING FOR A WALK was one of the major leisure pursuits before the First World War. Here, Joe Taylor, far left, and friend, Frank Walker, third from the right, rest for a while and look at the novelty of a cameraman. Cinema was in its infancy, the Lockwood Picture Palace being opened by the mayoress of Huddersfield on 18 November 1915. Silent pictures had been shown, however, in Huddersfield on 21 September 1896.

A GROUP OF HUDDERSFIELD GENTLEMEN, taking respite from work and not a smile among them. Second from the left is John Robinson, overlooker at a Whitacre Street mill. His wife's father, James Longbottom, was interested in herbs and nature. Frogs used to climb up the curtains in his home and hedgehogs were often to be seen beneath the dining-room table. Villagers often called there, at Woodend, Sheepridge, to have herbal medicines made up.

KATHLEEN DRIVER, (née Crowther) engaged in one of the finest leisure pursuits of all – reading in front of a crackling real fire with a dog to cuddle. A re-toucher at Dent's photographers at one time, Kathleen was for some years a member of Huddersfield Authors' Circle. Her family were brokers, of Primrose Hill. Before her death, Kathleen lived in a cottage at Dogley, Kirkburton, and collected antiques. In her will she left her home, Southfield, in grounds at Ravensknowle to be made into flats for the elderly after negotiating with Help the Aged.

DANCING TEACHER BLANCHE CHINN shows David Crawshaw how to tango? Her Sunday School scholars at Deighton in later years would never have associated Miss Chinn with anything as frivolous as dancing! Blanche taught dancing at Golcar Conservative Club and David was a councillor and JP, working in the goods department on the railway.

ROWLAND AND MABEL COOKE on a 'bicycle made for two' in 1925. Riding in a sidecar must have been somewhat hair-raising. In days when communication was not as easy as now, before the majority had telephones, patients in hospitals had numbers. The local paper, the *Huddersfield Examiner* printed which numbers at which hospitals were either 'dangerously' or 'seriously ill'. 'Relatives may visit' was sometimes added if the patient was well enough. In 1937 Mill Hill, Dalton, was still an isolation hospital.

MOST PEOPLE had neither cars, telephones, nor motor cycles and side-cars, so charabanc trips were their way of having a trip out. Dorothy Priestley is seen here in 1928 with William Taylor, market gardener, posing outside Ivy Coaches. Dorothy is wearing a then fashionable cloche hat.

'UNCLE ROB', entertainer, formerly of 8 Fleminghouse Lane, Waterloo, before moving to Fernside, Aldmondbury. Uncle Rob, or Mr Ward, enjoyed entertaining, especially the elderly.

JIMMY AINLEY was organist at the Picture House from 1943–55, and a regular customer at the Bull and Mouth. Playing the organ to packed cinema audiences was thirsty work! In the late forties and early fifties Jimmy also played for dances at Huddersfield Town Hall every Saturday evening.

HUDDERSFIELD PICTURE HOUSE, for sale in the 1950s. It opened at 19 Ramsden Street, on 26 December 1912. In 1939 the Home Office decreed that all places of amusement be closed. Later there was a relaxation of the ban and cinemas could be open until 10 p.m. On 30 July 1940 the cinemas were allowed to open on Sundays 'for soldiers and sailors and their friends'. Sunday opening of Huddersfield cinemas was allowed in 1941, with a plan for half to be opened one Sunday, and the remainder the following Sunday. The Picture House was the first building in Huddersfield specially erected for the exhibition of films.

Events

'SUCCESS TO OUR NEW STORES' is the slogan across the top of this CWS building, almost covered by bunting. Pelaw boot polishes, and bun flours, and Co-operative Wholesale Society's teas, coffees and cocoas are advertised along the top windows. Dawson, painter, is written on the small building to the right, and to the left on the tall bill board, 'This Land for Sale in Lots for building'. Even the gas lamp-standard is decorated at the top, and the two Co-op assistants in the doorway wear stiff white collars, ties, and long white aprons. On 24 November 1934 members of Huddersfield Industrial Society approved a £114,000 scheme for conversion of their central property into a 'walk round' store.

A NUMBER OF HUDDERSFIELD'S OUTLYING DISTRICTS followed the example of Longwood by holding an outdoor 'sing'. In August 1873, Jabez Iredale took men from Thornhill Reading Rooms at Longwood on to nearby hillside for a 'bit of a singalong'. At later 'sings' streets were blocked by wagonettes and cabs. Farnley Feast was held every Whitsuntide, and, among other attractions, young men vied with each other to climb a greasy pole to capture the leg of mutton at the top. Many children had their first introduction to music by being taken to the local 'sing', when musicians and villagers joined forces to swell the chorus of well-known hymns in the glorious outdoors.

'SUCCESS TO THE CHILDREN'S FESTIVAL'. How proudly the little dog sits on the buffet in the centre of the group. They appear quite a melancholy group considering it was a festival.

Pleasure Ground, Hope Bank Pleasure Gardens, Honley Nr.Huddersfield.

HOPE BANK PLEASURE GARDENS, founded by J.W. Mellor in 1893. Those who could not afford a seaside holiday took delight in a trip to Hope Bank. There were 'Curiosities of all kinds – magic mirrors which cause roars of laughter'; boating on the lake 'with careful attendants'; a large dancing stage and accommodation for thousands, wet or fine. Weddings, Picnics and Junior Leagues were specially catered for. A bear escaped once, causing much consternation at Honley. Brook Motors is now where Hope Bank used to be. Harold Mellor, a descendant of the founder, has the Nursery Garden at Aldmondbury.

A BIG OCCASION – all dressed up for a family group photograph. Identification on the back, reads: 'Uncle George Aldred' who worked at W.C. Holmes, 'Aunt Beatie', Aunt Florrie, Aunt Ethel and children.

THE WEDDING OF LIONEL PROCTOR at St James' Church, Slaithwaite on 27 September 1905.
The bridegroom's family had an ironwork business. The then twenty-five-year-old Elinor
Hirst was the bride, daughter of Schofield Hirst, insurance agent of Varley Road, Slaithwaite.
Lionel was the son of Thomas Alexander Proctor and was twenty-eight years old. Cloth
presser Thomas Edward Clark is on the left. In the 1860s 'Slawit Spa' was the Harrogate of
the district. The first Wednesday in May was the opening day of the baths. The elite of the
Colne Valley were on view, and a bachelor gentleman from Golcar led the open air ball on
the Green.

THE CONCERT, *WISHING CAP*, probably given at Deighton in 1923. Lena Thomas is kneeling at the front, and Dorothy Priestley left, with tinsel falling down her forehead. Also in the photograph are Bella Rice, Annie Mary Charlesworth, Madge Clayton, Mary Dyson, Ernest Taylor, Ben Pearson (lying down, far right), Johnnie Walton, Wright Charlesworth (lying down, far left), George Hartley in smock, Marjorie Crawshaw, Nora and Eileen Oddy. Bessie Whitehead played Isabella.

A SHOW put on by High Street Methodist in December 1912 was *The Chinese Girls' School*. The gas showroom is now where the chapel used to be. Huddersfield Glee and Madrigal Society had a special concert in the Town Hall on Saturday 11 September 1886. Mr Herbert Haigh sang 'Love Sounds the Alarm' from *Acis and Galatea*. Male voices sang the Soldiers' Chorus from *Faust*, and the glee, 'When Evening's twilight', some of the contributions. Admission cost: area 1s., balcony (reserved) 1s. 6d., back seats and gallery 6d., children under fourteen half price to all parts.

JANET ROBINSON (later Mrs Whyte) who worked as a tailoress at Bairstows stands far right. Later she went to Southport as third companion to a rich lady. However, there was an awesome statue of Venus in the bedroom 'glaring at her' so she decided to return to Huddersfield and live with her sister Clara at Sheepridge! What magnificent hats – they would surely grace Ascot, let alone Huddersfield.

DORIS FRANCE IN BERET, far left, at a garden party in 'Coddy' Taylor's market garden. Doris lived at 14 Clifton Terrace, Deighton, and was a mender at William Thomson & Sons. Marjorie Crawshaw, sitting on a wall, fell into one of the greenhouses in 1923, and 'Coddy' often chased youngsters who were pinching apples from the orchard.

FOUR GENERATIONS are photographed together in William Taylor's Market Garden in Deighton. Grandma Taylor is far right, Harry Gibson is at the front with his mother Lizzie standing behind, Aunt Betsy is on the left. There were many greenhouses. William, John, and Law were brothers. Law Taylor was the first Labour mayor of Huddersfield in the 1920s, with hugely different political views to his brothers.

THIS PHOTOGRAPH WAS ON A POSTCARD, posted from Elland in October 1905 to 'Mifs Lodge, Whitehead Lane, Primrose Hill'. The dog looks like Turk, who belonged to Kathleen Crowther. The nursemaid on the left is holding a bunch of snowdrops. Antimacassar on the couch is typical of all the precautions taken in those days to protect furniture from dust.

A GARDEN PARTY AT MAYFIELD, Ashenhurst, in 1920 to raise funds for Primrose Hill Baptist chapel. On the left of the back row are Doris Waddington, Mollie Halstead and Nellie Sykes. Seated far left is Dorothy Atha (Bo-Peep); the 'nurse' was Elsie Barker; sailor, Hugh Thomas. Also in the photograph is Roy Porteus.

A CONCERT AT DEIGHTON. Mabel Priestley, standing third left on the middle row, holds the hand of the kneeling girl in the centre. Also pictured are Kitty Walker, Ethel Waring, and Hilda Bates.

HERE THEY GO AGAIN, showing off at Deighton. At least with concert rehearsals so frequent, children were hardly ever bored, and there was perhaps less mischief about in those early years. Creative outlets were the order of the day. The gentleman was Walter Wibberley.

HUDDERSFIELD AND DISTRICT YOUNG CONSERVATIVES in 'A Spectacular Musical Play in Two Acts' produced by Madame Elsie Stringer and performed in St Patrick's Hall on 17 March 1931. Left to right: Edith Crawshaw, Evelyn Berry, W. Sykes, E. Lowell, Dorothy Priestley, M. Hobson, E. Jagger, S. Dunnill, and Leonora Shaw. Leonora played the part of Cora Bellamy.

HAVING A PHOTOGRAPH TAKEN was too much for the poor little infant covering her eyes in the middle of the front row! A neighbourhood group taken at Kidroyd, Moldgreen. Looks of suspicion and amazement predominate, and how about the almost adult type hat on the baby seated on the knee of the lady wearing a shawl over her head. . .?

A TRAM ACCIDENT, Bradley, 22 April 1905. Trams first ran on a Sunday in Huddersfield on 9 June 1901. How that must have offended some, who believed that no work should be done on the Sabbath! Besides the 'Hovis Bread' advert ('Adds a Charm to Every Meal'), H. Roebuck of Moldgreen and Buxton Road advertised on the tram – 'Furnish for Cash or Credit'.

THE WEDDING OF HILDA GREGORY AND ARTHUR HULME in August 1935. They then lived in Lockwood House, Lockwood. Sydney Gregory, the bride's brother, is to her right; sister Doris, who never married, and their mother Mrs Buckley who married twice are on the far right. Huddersfield elegance in the thirties was promoted by such establishments as Beatrice Stephenson Ltd, 46 John William Street; Madame Lucette, 56 John William Street. For men who dressed smartly, Ben Pearson, 6–8 Brook's Yard, Market Street, was the place to buy clothes.

AFTER ONE HAPPY EVENT . . . there follows another. Doris Gregory holds the new baby, Sylvia, after her christening in 1936. Next to her, on the right, Hilda smilingly relinquishes maternal responsibilites for a brief time. Proud dad Arthur stands behind her. Uncle Syd tries to draw nephew Peter's attention to the photographer, his wife Doris in floppy 'thirties' hat is next to them. Doris unfortunately died from pernicious anaemia and her baby died shortly after birth. Hilda later gave birth to Christine and finally Arthur. Arthur, who first worked for Karrier Motors, became a foreman at Brown's Tractors, Meltham.

THE OLD FOLKS' TREAT, Thornton Lodge Methodist church, 1950. Eighty-seven-year-old Fanny France, head down, is on the second row from the front at the left. Her sister Janet Whyte is next to her wearing spectacles, then seventy-seven, but how about the pact – ten years off their ages?

ANOTHER OLD FOLKS' TREAT, this time at either Moldgreen or Dalton. The Revd Ogden, wearing his dog collar, is on the left. Joseph Ogden, then of 150 Penistone Road, Waterloo, celebrated his ninetieth birthday in 1955 at the central YMCA. He had been in the Methodist ministry for sixty-two years.

A HARVEST FESTIVAL AT FARNLEY TYAS. Probably not the disastrous one of 1896, when the vicar refused to hold a thanksgiving service in the church, so George Eastwood decided to conduct a service in the bar parlour of the Golden Cock. Some of the rotting sheaves were gathered and brought to the inn, and George recited a burlesque 'hymn' which he had composed for the occasion. Entitled 'Day of Humiliation, Confessions and Lamentations' it mockingly censured the villagers for their 'daily sins and conduct base' and accused them of paying more attention to eating and drinking than to work in the fields. There was a plea for 'grace and pardon' in the concluding verse, and expectations of 'filled barns' next harvest.

CHILDREN OF TOWN AVENUE, Turnbridge, Castlegate area celebrate the silver jubilee of King George V and Queen Mary in 1935 with a street party. Maisie Durkin, back row, brought her doll to the party. On the back row: Arthur Gill, the tall boy; Bill Hampshire, far left; Tony Firth, second from the left. Bill O'Hara in the white hat is at the front. Schoolchildren were presented with a spoon in a box lying on blue velvet, and a 'silver' tin of chocolate with the royal couple's portrait.

SOME PHOTOGRAPHER was determined to make a record of the 'happy' silver jubilee day for these Town Avenue and Hillhouse District youngsters. Mrs Chapman watches from the gate. John O'Hara is far right at back, Dominic Durkin next to him. Maisie Durkin kneels, by herself, at the back. Also pictured are Vera Rowsel and Eddie, and Arthur Gill. The little girl with the doll on the front row seems anything but happy with the photographer!

NO SILVER JUBILEE would have been possible without the king and queen, and no party without these ladies! Left to right: Winnie O'Hara, Mrs Durkin, Mrs Quinn, Mrs Gill, Mrs Firth, Mrs Webster, Mrs Chadwick, Mrs Woodhouse, Mrs Chapman, Mrs Clayton and Mrs Shaw. Mrs O'Hara worked at her mother-in-law's lodging house in Castlegate as a cleaner.

HERE ARE THE DADS joining in the silver jubilee street party. Front left: Messrs Chapman, Clayton, Quinn, O'Hara, Chadwick. Back row, second left, Mr Woodhouse; third, Mr Shaw; fourth, Mr Webster, -?-, Mr Durkin, and Mr Gill far right. Mr Firth said grace before the party began, and 'God bless the king and queen' before all tucked into the Shippams fish-paste sandwiches.

A PERFORMANCE OF *MISS HOOK OF HOLLAND* at Hepworth Methodist chapel. Muriel Kelly is in the second row back, fourth right, standing, wearing a check skirt. The show took place in 1949 or thereabouts. By this time more than 'locals' could get to shows put on at outlying places such as Hepworth. At the Wheel School of Motoring, 43 Westgate, Huddersfield, in 1955, learning to drive cost 17s. 6d. per lesson, or a full twelve hour course, £10 10s. Also in the photograph are: Kenneth Turner, Helen Haigh, Shirley Dickinson, Raymond Haigh, Barbara Kaye, David Shaw, Jenny Moorhouse, John England. Tutor was Madame F. Barrett of Holmfirth.

BIBLE PATTERN FELLOWSHIP GROUP prior to leaving Huddersfield by Hanson's Excursion Coach, to hear evangelist Billy Graham. Bryan Cooke stands, far left, next to Ada Truelove. Ada's sister Edith is holding a handbag.

AFTER SPIRITUAL REFRESHMENT, some more down-to-earth food for the Bible Fellowship. Bryan Cooke is far left with Ada Truelove next to him in the foreground, smiling for the photographer. Ada now lives in Elland, Bryan, in Thornton Lodge. Bible Pattern met in Dundas Street, Huddersfield. Their pastor was David Heywood.

MRS NORA KITSON, instigator of the 1964 Denby Dale Pie, standing in the 18 ft long, 6 ft wide, 1 ft 6 in deep dish. Prior to the big day, the dish was registered as a ship, the SS *Denby Dale*, and dignitaries went for a sail on the Mirfield canal. The night after the sail, someone sank the pie dish, but worse things had happened at previous big pie days. The one baked to celebrate Queen Victoria's jubilee in 1887 was bad, and the terrible aroma sent people scurrying away. It was buried in quick-lime in Toby Wood. Some still possess memorial cards to the pie.

MRS IVY BROADBENT, MRS SUSAN RICHARDSON AND MRS SHAW selling souvenir Pie Plates on 5 September 1964. I think they cost 7s. 6d. each, but now they are collectors' items. Mrs Shaw is the grandmother of Ruth Lawrence, the mathematics genius who lived on Halifax Old Road prior to gaining early admission to Oxford University. Both Mrs Shaw and Mrs Richardson were members of Huddersfield Authors' Circle. Mrs Broadbent lives at Greenhead Lane, Dalton.

PHILIP HARBEN, ONE OF THE EARLY TV COOKS, (far left, bearded) joins the Mayor and Mayoress of Huddersfield and other people awaiting the arrival of the giant pie in 1964. The 1928 pie took nearly 1½ days to bake, and refused to come out of the oven. It was eventually levered out with large steel tram rails and took twenty local men to get it into position. At its destination, Inkerman Park, speeches were made, then Mr Wood used carvers one yard long to attack the crust.

COOKS AND ASSISTANTS await the arrival of the VIP, the 1964 giant Denby Dale pie. Portions of pie cost half a crown each. Lots of cardboard containers were lined up to serve them on. Entertainment included brass bands, traditional dancing by the Grenoside Morris Men and marching displays. At 3.05 p.m. the pie was blessed and the cutting ceremony was performed by Jonas Kenyon.

DENBY DALE made the 1928 'Biggest Pie in the World' in order to raise money to endow a cot in Huddersfield Royal Infirmary. Between 20,000 and 30,000 partook of the pie. It contained four bullocks, 600 lb beef, 15 cwt potatoes, 80 st flour, 2 cwt lard, 2 st baking powder. It weighed 45 cwt. The dish was steel and weighed 35 cwt, totalling about 4 tons. The village was fully decorated for the event, as though for a coronation.

THE NAME EDITH WOOD is written on the back of this photograph of a concert group. So, beneath the disguises, Edith must be there somewhere. Either a Moldgreen or Deighton event I think.

'NEPTUNE'S DAUGHTER' CONTEST at the Ritz cinema, Friday 28 April 1950. Prizes for the winner included a large bouquet of Spring flowers, a month's free pass for two to the cinema, a box of fruit squashes, and a 'Tony' home perm outfit. The competition was in connection with a film of the same name.

A PARTY JUST FOR THE SAKE OF ONE, at 41 Avison Road, Cowlersley, in 1950. With none having a car, what a lot of bus trips into town were needed to buy in all the food; Supper was enjoyed by candlelight, for an extra romantic atmosphere.

HUDDERSFIELD ELOCUTIONIST SHIELA HINCHLIFFE was bridesmaid for National Provincial Bank employees Philip Taylor and Audrey Cudworth at Bradley Church, 5 July 1949. Brides-maids' dresses were from Beatrice Stephenson's; the reception was at Whiteley's Café, Westgate. From left to right: Bob Jackson, Sheila Hinchliffe, Carol Halstead, Philip and Audrey, the bride's uncle, Hazel Taylor and Leslie Moorhouse.

WILLIAM COUSINS and family. Baby Phyllis is in the pram.

FINALS OF HUDDERSFIELD SUMMER ENTERTAINMENTS TALENT CONTEST, Greenhead Park, Saturday 20 August 1960. Paul Lockwood, who sang 'The Holy City' won the Frank Jordan Cup. Mr G. Whitwam was organizer and compère, Mr R. Oxley the accompanist. Dancing teacher Nora Bray presented 'Follies On Parade' at the opening in the Open Air Theatre on 16 July.

HILDA TAYLOR, when Miss Haigh, used to work at Flack's, Market Walk. The proprietor of Flack's, ladies' outfitters, used to allow her to wear a fur outside occasionally, as long as she told everyone where it came from. A means of advertising in the 1920s.

Schools

THESE CHILDREN were either having playtime or drill at Stile Common School. One of the teachers in the playground may be Annie Whitworth. Drill later became PT. Talking in class was often punished by pupils being made to keep their hands on top of their heads for a period of time. The 'nit nurse' was almost as frequent a visitor as infectious diseases. John M. Gibson was chief school medical officer in April 1931. That month a circular was sent to schools containing advice on common infectious and contagious diseases of school children. After listing symptoms of scarlet fever, measles, diptheria and the others, teachers were advised to make sure all children kept to their own pencils (so many sucked the pencil ends to aid the mental process) and 'slates should not be used', as in early school days some scholars used spit as a quick cleaning method for slates.

A CLASS AT MOLDGREEN SCHOOL in the early 1920s. Included in the group: Mary Cousins, Nora Goldsbrough, Mabel Beaumont, Mary Ely. The museum being near, classes sometimes went there for lessons. Girls did country dancing, but never with the boys. Stool ball was frequently played. A favourite after school game was playing 'ghosts' around Asquith's grocery shop. Mary Cousins used to chant 'I am the Ghost of the Crimson Raspberries. . .'

THIS MAY BE AN EARLY DEIGHTON COUNCIL OR 'BOARD' SCHOOL CLASS. In 1886 children paid 2d. a week if infants, 3d. standard I, 4d. standards II and III, 5d. for IV, V and VI. Half timers paid 3d. Under the Education Act of 1870 small grants towards teachers' salaries were available, but it was still necessary to charge 'pence' to augment the sums. There were no half term holidays in early days, just a week at Christmas, Easter, and Whitsuntide, and three weeks in midsummer.

G. HOLDSWORTH & CO, PHOTOGRAPHER, Moldgreen, certainly did not believe in making the school children say 'cheese' when posing. The boy on the front, far right, holds a board with the school's name, but it is too faded to read. Even the two boys holding cricket bats on the back row cannot muster a smile. The school may be Paddock. Perhaps a few faces may be recognized?

A HUDDERSFIELD SCHOOL GROUP, probably in the 1920s. Children usually made their own amusements in those days. Sledges were made out of old pram wheels, a plank of wood and a length of rope for steering.

A SCHOOL GROUP in the early years of the century. The footwear on the front row looks uncomfortably sturdy, even that of the girls. In the days before the National Health Service, some could not afford a doctor when their children were ill. But Dr MacGregor of Rashcliffe, and one or two others, excused payment by such people. Dentists sometimes bribed patients with a penny for not crying.

A DEIGHTON COUNCIL SCHOOL CLASS NATURE RAMBLE to Newhouse Wood in 1926. Reggie Priestley, son of choirmaster Arthur, is far right, behind the two girls at the front. An assortment of leaves and flowers were gathered and taken back to school where facts about them were written up in 'jotters'. I wonder if anyone still has any of those old pressed leaves and flowers? The photographer was teacher Miss Gaunt.

LINTHWAITE C OF E INFANTS CLASS, 1924. Harriet Wood (now Mrs Bailey), wearing a ribbon, is on the second row from the back, fourth child from right. Miss Marshall is on the left, and Mrs Spinks, far right. If only this picture could speak — it would probably tell of canings, and knuckles often red raw, according to Harriet. She never missed school once in nine years. Soon after Linthwaite church was built in 1828, it was thought a school should be built where children could be taught to read and write, and learn their catechism, and the Church's teaching of spiritual and moral values. In 1830 a school, one large room and a smaller classroom for infants, came into being. As public opinion and legislation began to limit the time and age of children working in factories it became possible to open weekday schools. Linthwaite had its first National Day School in 1866 with the appointment of Mr Edward Bland as headmaster.

SOME PUPILS OF GREENHEAD HIGH SCHOOL in the mid-1920s. The headmistress was Miss Annie Hill, thirteenth right on the mistresses' row. French mistress Miss New is sixth from the left in a white blouse. Ninth from the left is Beatrice Beard with short hair and fringe, who taught biology. Miss Bucke, who taught maths, is sixth from the right. Muriel Cheetham, now Mrs Jessop, is fourteenth from the right on the back row. One old girl recalls her attempt to make a pair of knickers in domestic science. Miss Hill scathingly read out that Mildred Taylor had only ten marks in the exam. When the domestic science mistress saw Mildred, she informed her she had not really earned any marks. If her 'block' had been made up, the resulting pair of knickers would have had seven legs! It was rumoured that in 1918, when Queen Mary spoke to the head girl, Gladys Cotton, she enquired to which orphanage the girls belonged! Girls received gifts of chocolate and fountain pens to commemorate the jubilee of King George V in 1935. Head girl Joan Milnes (1938/9) became one of Huddersfield's best known veterinary surgeons. House names were St Hilda (love of learning); St Clare (care for those in need); Montrose – the Earl of Montrose, loyalty to the King, and Gordon (responsibility for backward peoples).

A GROUP OF GREENHEAD HIGH SCHOOL GIRLS in a play, possibly the *Merchant of Venice* which was performed by members of the Dramatic Society in May 1911. In the school magazine of that year it was remarked that the staging of the woodland scene earned well-merited applause. Proceeds of the three performances after expenses were paid, amounted to £9 13s. 9d., of which £3 13s. 9d. was granted to the Kyrle Society, and £1 to the gardening fund. With the remaining £5 head lights and curtains were to be bought, and the balance kept in hand to defray expense of books and clothes for the following year.

HILLHOUSE CENTRAL SCHOOL in 1915. Pupils were later transferred to Longley Hall. Mr Montgomery was headmaster, to the left of him is Gertrude Jessop and Ethel Dews to the right. Dorothy Atha is on the second row from the back, second from the left. She was vice-captain at Longley. Form captain Gladys Griffiths is on the back row, second right. The school song was 'Forty Years On'.

BRYAN COOKE smilingly obliges the school photographer in 1939. When big cities were thought to be immediate bombing targets at the outbreak of war that year, some Bradford children were sent to Kirkburton. When fears of Bradford's being bombed were allayed a few months afterwards, the children soon went back home. Bryan attended Knowl Bank school, Golcar. Blanche Chinn taught him there; she also taught at Paddock school.

LAST DAY OF TERM FOR DALTON JUNIOR SCHOOL, July 1965. Carolyn Jackson is at the back, Jill Senior is on the far right, Diane Hill(?) far left, and Caroline Wheeler at the front, looking forward to becoming a Greenhead High School girl in the autumn.

ANOTHER LINTHWAITE C OF E CLASS in 1924. It was not until 1874 that the Slaithwaite Gas Co. laid mains through Roydhouse up to the church; until that time the elementary school was illuminated by oil lamps. In 1926 conversion of outside toilets to a water carriage system and the installation of two toilets inside the school was carried out at a cost of £520 13s. 1d. The cost was met by the Church. School was divided into standards, I being the lowest, VII the highest. To move from one standard to another, an examination had to be passed. A few who kept failing could spend their entire school life in Standard I. There were no school dinners, and everyone walked to and from school. Talking during lessons was not allowed, and to obtain permission to speak a child had to put a hand up and ask. If anyone talked and was seen, they were either kept in at hometime or had to stand on a form with hands on head.

The 1940s

BESIDES THE WAR, the forties were marked by extreme weather and deep snowfalls, especially in 1947. Arthur Littlewood died at this time and the ordinary hearse was unable to reach Holmfirth cemetery because of deep snowdrifts. Harry Lee, quarry worker, in the bowler hat, strains every sinew to drag the weight of the sledge towards the cemetery, the only means of transporting it.

STALWART GENTLEMEN, correctly dressed even in those atrocious conditions, drag the coffin to its final resting place, making it almost like a scene from the modern *Last of the Summer Wine.*

NEARLY THERE, and bowler-hatted mourners can be seen negotiating drifts in between the gravestones behind the main party. One might even say that in such weather it was probably better to be under the ground than above it.

HARRY CLIFFE, amateur photographer, of Mirfield, snapped Hazel and Joe Taylor, with Major, on 23 January 1946. Animals, who did not have to venture further than their own garden, enjoyed the novelty of snow. That evening John Garfield was at the Ritz in *Forever in Love*. The following week *Gaslight* was at the Theatre Royal. On 9 February there was a Home Guard dance at Cambridge Road Baths. After a show, Lindon Smith's for a fish and chip supper was an enjoyable finalé to an evening.

MAJOR THE LABRADOR AND HAZEL TAYLOR visit Jeanne Wood at 29 Woodhouse Avenue in the big snow of 1947. Riding macs were popular. When grubby, they had to be scrubbed clean in the bath. The fur hat was concocted out of an ancient fur; these were still 'make do and mend' days. A diary entry for 7 March 1947 mentioned going to a dance at Cambridge Road – 'awful trying to keep long dress out of the snow'. Sometimes people had to walk on walls, since roads could not be seen for drifts of snow. Walking to work became a social occasion, everyone teaming up to negotiate the drifts.

DAMAGE CAUSED BY FLOOD THROUGH CLOUDBURST ON WHIT-MONDAY, MAY 29th, 1944. SHOWING COLLAPSE OF MARKET WALK, HOLMFIRTH.

ON WHIT MONDAY, 29 May 1944 it was very hot. In the afternoon there was a vicious thunder storm. The cloudburst had devastating effects, and the photograph shows some of them. However, in traditional style the 'show had to go on' and Joan Hammond sang at the Theatre Royal. It was worth putting on our raincoats to go and see and hear her!

DAMAGE CAUSED BY FLOOD THROUGH CLOUDBURST ON WHIT-MONDAY, MAY 29th, 1944. ACTUAL FLOOD IN HOLLOWGATE, HOLMFIRTH, SHOWING CHURCH AFTER SHOPS HAD COLLAPSED.

ANOTHER VIEW OF THE CLOUDBURST DAMAGE at Holmfirth. Any chapel 'marchers' in traditional processions must have been absolutely soaked.

WINIFRED HALSTEAD WITH BROTHER ERNIE HAIGH, killed while serving in the tank corps in 1942. Mrs Halstead had the arts and crafts shop on Byram Street at the time. Ernie wrote a diary in Dunkirk: 'Out of the very heart of the sunset steamed a long line of ships with pennants flying in the evening breeze. Someone cheered, it was taken up by three thousand – then singing, "Land of Hope and Glory". A voice said ... "Let us pray". Men knelt and covered their faces with their hands. "Oh merciful Father, who of thy Gracious Mercy hath seen fit to deliver these thy soldiers out of a great tribulation, grant that they may be ever worthy of thy care for them. Through Jesus Christ our Lord, Amen."'

GRANVILLE WHEELER, from Lowestwood, Linthwaite, in the Signals during the Second World War. Part of his service was in Münster Lager, Germany, in 1946. The following year saw him and colleagues shovelling snow from the A1 at Catterick. The only bit of warmth was in the toilets, where a stove was kept burning to try and stop them freezing up. There was no heating in the living quarters of the soldiers because of coal shortages – some was taken to married quarters. On demob a brown suit, trilby hat and shoes were provided.

AUDREY ARMITAGE, of Netherton, photographed in the forties by 'Polyfoto'. Audrey was a pupil of Greenhead High School and later worked at the Halifax Building Society in Cloth Hall Street. There was a confectioner's in the arcade opposite, and staff used to send the junior across for custards and jam tarts for mid-morning break. They were a bit on the hard side, due to wartime food shortages, but quite a bit of squabbling ensued if what had been ordered did not materialize! Here, Audrey wears her hair in a typical forties style. The 'Liberty Cut' was favoured by others, or the Pageboy style. Those on munitions wore 'snoods' to keep hair from catching in machinery.

JUNE HARRIES, formerly of Sheepridge, who joined the WAAF and was stationed at RAF Padgate. A former pupil of Kaye's College, New North Road, June loved to attend dances at Cambridge Road when home on leave. Double summertime added to the magic of life in Huddersfield in the 1940s. Walking home beneath a moonlit sky with a dashing Canadian, Polish, or other young man newly arrived in Huddersfield was so romantic. Some girls did marry GIs and other men they would never have encountered in the normal course of events.

PRINCE, HILDA AND HAZEL TAYLOR, wearing an RAF badge on the coat lapel, photographed by Geoffrey's studio on 9 June 1942. Not many had cameras then and, if they did, film was difficult to get, so if a family pet was to be remembered it had to be taken to a studio. Life for both animals and humans during the war was in some ways more easy going than today. There was no specially tinned food for animals; they gratefully gobbled up what was left on plates after humans had finished. Usually, plates were simply put on the floor for them to 'clean up'.

EDITH MCLOUGHLIN, left, and her mother outside their home at No. 54 Bentley Street, Lockwood, during the 1940s. A dirndl skirt was worn by Edith. Bentley Street was named after Robert Bentley, wealthy landowner and part owner of Lockwood Brewery. Edith attended Greenhead High School in the 1940s and when not overwhelmed with homework, enjoyed dancing at Fox's in Trinity Street.

IT MIGHT HAVE BEEN WARTIME, but that did not mean slovenly dressing. Margaret Wheeler, of Lowestwood, Linthwaite, here wears a 'halo' hat, fashionable at the time, as a wedding guest. Rodney Armitage is the essence of schoolboy smartness. Margaret worked at Rushworths.

A WEDDING GROUP in the 1940s. The lady in the foreground is Marie Wood, with Waldo Kenworthy. Evelyn Wood is far left, with Mrs Mavis Armitage. Some confectioners used cardboard imitation 'icing' when sugar was in short supply. Friends and relations generously gave some of their clothing coupons to help a bride buy some sort of trousseau. Those who could afford it frequented cafés to save their food ration. If you had soup and a main course, however, you were barred from having a dessert. Or a customer was not allowed to spend more then five shillings on a meal. Some simply went into another establishment to finish off their meal.

JIMMY WOOD (RIGHT), OF RIDDINGS ROAD, with a friend, wearing waistcoats with suits, everyday wear for those not in uniform during the forties. Jimmy used to do odd jobs to help out, and amused those who employed him with his stories. Once, he said, he was late because he had been 'fast asleep under t'table listening to t' wireless'. Frequently he wore a white silk muffler, to do away with the nuisance of wearing a tie. The lady shoppers in the photograph are all wearing hats. How different the cars were then, and how few there were.

WARTIME FASHIONS WERE SMART, especially if you could 'wangle' more clothing coupons. Hilda Taylor, living at a shop, was in that fortunate position. Some customers, with more children than they could really afford, sold their clothing coupons to those who would buy. 'Black Market' perhaps, but it suited all concerned. The grocer swapped surplus with the butcher and vice versa. A flour traveller even smuggled a sack of white flour into Central Stores one wartime Christmas. It was hidden in a bedroom and kept for special occasions. Such a delicacy after the National Loaf!

WARTIME SHORTAGES certainly made people use their initiative. Mrs Jessop, of Woodhouse Avenue, Fartown, cooled off in an old bath in her back garden in the absence of garden furniture. Girls made blouses out of parachute silk and belts from plaited cellophane. Some townspeople bought siren suits to wear in the Anderson shelters if the sirens shrilled. Most threw old coats on. One family used to play Monopoly in their cellar until the 'all clear' rang out. Others said 'if my name's on it I can't do anything about it' (meaning the bomb) — and stayed in bed.

BETTY KEY, OF BRADFORD ROAD, land girl on a Meltham farm during the war. She had to be up with the larks, winter and summer, but it did not stop her jiving and quick-stepping the nights away. Greenhead Masonic, the Co-op Hall and Town Hall were other popular dance halls.

RONNIE BOOTH, a well-known Huddersfield drummer. Here he is when drumming for the Squadronnaires at Butlin's, Filey, in 1948. Ronnie lives in Meltham, and still enjoys entertaining on the drums.

AUB HIRST'S WESTBOURNE PLAYERS, at Cambridge Road Baths, 1941. Ronnie Booth is on the drums. Big Band names who visited during the war included Oscar Rabin, Victor Sylvester, and Ken Mackintosh.

RONNIE BOOTH is at the back on drums. Roy Beverley is at the back on the right. He lost a leg in a motor cycle accident – which did nothing to diminish the adoration he received from Huddersfield girls. Aub Hirst is at the front, right, his brother Fred, left. This was Saturday night at the Baths, 10 February 1944.

AUB HIRST'S WESTBOURNE PLAYERS, Cambridge Road Baths, 1941. Roland Iredale, bass; Sam Brierly, piano; Ronnie Booth, drums. Also pictured are: Harry Mercer, Brian Tann, Aub and Fred Hirst and Lewis Hill. Remember some of those tunes: 'One O'Clock Jump', 'Crazy Rhythm', 'I Can't Give You Anything But Love', 'Young and Healthy', 'Little Brown Jug'...? Thirsty dancers could have their hands rubber stamped as a 'pass out' to enable them to visit the Sportsman pub. Cloakroom tickets cost twopence.

Childhood

AT FIRST GLANCE one would think these little girls feeding the ducks in Beaumont Park in 1930 included the then 'Little Princesses', Elizabeth and Margaret Rose. Most parents at that time copied the type of clothes worn by them for their own children, particularly for 'best' outfits which were only worn on Sundays, and then with strict instructions not to get them dirty. These are sisters Joyce, Edith, and Hetty McLoughlin, then living on Bentley Street, Lockwood, enjoying the after Sunday School treat of a visit to the park. No self-respecting young lady of any age was to be seen without a hat and 'Cherry Blossomed' shining shoes in the thirties.

WHAT A THRILL when Edith McLoughlin was presented with a wooden motor car by great uncle Joseph in 1931! Big enough to ride in, round Stanley Street, Milner Street, and her own Bentley Street, Lockwood. Big sister, Joyce, hands on hips, stands proudly behind.

A WELL-EARNED REST on a park bench after feeding the ducks for Hetty McLoughlin with Muriel Campbell, Edith and Joyce McLoughlin. White 'tennis' socks, black patent ankle straps, a new dress and bonnet, possibly from Kaye's Drapers, of King Street, made Whit Sunday a highlight of the year for small girls in the 1930s. In the late thirties Joyce McLoughlin worked as a manageress at Longwood Co-op drapers.

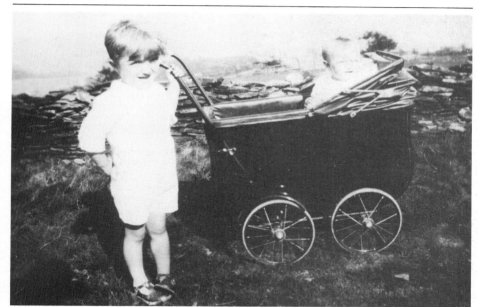

GORDON COUSINS in charge of pram in 1930, with baby Kenneth looking out. He is pictured on Bank End Lane, 'Ready Money Row', Aldmondbury. Jackson's Furnishing Stores, 5 Queen Street, sold prams like this at £3 12s. 6d. or 1s. 6d. weekly in 1935. Babyfair, 15 Queen Street, also sold prams and other nursery equipment.

WHAT WILL THE FUTURE HOLD? Little Kenneth Cousins, in a cap with a popular 'pom-pom' at the side and black shiny patent shoes, is in contemplative mood at Aldmondbury Bank, in the 1930s. He became a master joiner and cabinet maker and now lives at Hall Bower.

KENNETH COUSINS AND GORDON in Sunday best on Aldmondbury Bank, 1933. The gentleman striding out, left, is wearing the usual outfit of flat cap, white shirt, tweed jacket and flannel 'bags'. The horse, over the wall, looks as though he is about to enter the open doorway. Fred Wood, 'the Hatter' opposite the tramway offices in town advertised 'All the latest styles in Gents' Hats, caps and hosiery' around this time.

GRACE FIRTH visiting her grandad's home in Gipsy Row (Greenhead Lane) Dalton in the 1930s. Brian Firth and Kenneth Cousins keep warm in fashionable angora fluffy hats pulled well down over the ears. Gordon Cousins and Geoffrey Firth (who later became a doctor) are smartly dressed in schoolboy caps, ties and overcoats, and are standing behind with Grace.

ADA TRUELOVE used to take an Oxo cube to Woodhouse school. For her dinner, boiling water was poured on it. One Christmas Herbert, her father, determined his daughter should have a toy. He had been given an old fur coat by an elderly lady who he pushed out in her bassinet. Herbert cut the best parts out and fashioned a bear, with boot buttons for eyes. He hung it over Ada's bed. When she awoke that Christmas morning, she realized that it was supposed to be a toy of some sort, and carried it around with her for a long time. Another time the teacher ordered her to take off her coat, but she could not, for there was nothing underneath. Such poverty did not make Ada bitter, as she 'had, and still has, trust in the Lord'.

A GROUP OF FIRST WORLD WAR HUDDERSFIELD SCHOOLBOYS playing at soldiers, and looking forward to joining up. At school, children wrote on slates at this time. Marbles were popular as were whips and tops, shuttle cocks, and climbing trees and lamp-posts. Some contrived to make stilts out of empty treacle tins with two long sticks of wood stuck inside.

MABEL AND DORIS FRANCE 'playing out'. In those days districts around Huddersfield were far more rural, with lots to interest children in the hedgerows and fields. Those voluminous pinafores, ostensibly to keep dresses clean, must have taken ages to launder. The little girls' socks appear to be hand-knitted.

A YOUNGER KATHLEEN CROWTHER, probably wondering how on earth she will get out of all those clothes, photographed on a wicker chair covered with a rug. Kathleen was born in December 1908. She lived with her grandad, Robert Lodge, and her mother at the broker's house and shop. 'Bits and pieces' of household goods were always on view outside.

A CHILDREN'S CONCERT, given by Moldgreen Methodist church, probably in 1913. Mary Moss is on the far left, Mary Cousins with a frilly cap holds a teddy bear at the back. Magic lantern shows were soon to make way for silent films. I wonder it any of these youngsters saw the first Charlie Chaplin film in the Victoria Hall, Huddersfield, on 23 November 1914?

GEORGE HAROLD BRUMMIT with his wooden 'booler'. Village shops used to have hoops hanging up by the door outside. Some enterprising dads could make the toys themselves, at no cost. Girls had wooden hoops. George, still young enough not to wear boys' clothing, would not be considered big enough to take charge of an iron hoop with iron hook to steer it over the cobbled streets. In Victorian days it was said that the hoop represented the Wheel of Fortune and that 'its roundness instructs us that there is no end to man's care and toil'.

GROWING UP. Mabel, left, and sister Doris France in broderie anglais dresses. George Hall's, of King Street, Huddersfield, for Whitsuntide 1912 advertised 'Ladies black satin, chiffon, taffeta, voile, and lace coats. Nemo, Worths, La Fleur, and Child's Rational Corsets. Prices from 1s. 9½d. to 35s. 9d. Also Ready to Wear Mourning Wear, Sunshades, Paris Jewellery'. At Queen Street Mission that Whitsuntide, over 600 scholars and friends went by train to Kirkburton to a field at Tenter Flatts, Highburton. Oranges were given to the children through the kindness of 'two friends'. The usual games were played, and tea was served in the field for scholars, and in the primitive Methodist schoolroom for friends.

OUTSIDE A COTTAGE, HILL TOP. A 'Kate Greenaway' type outfit is worn here by Kathleen Crowther, relaxing in a rocking chair with her dog, Turk. Even he has a mat of his own to sit on. The early part of the twentieth century is represented by the round door knob, fancy cloth on the table and what appears to be an aspidistra plant.

THE THREE CHILDREN OF HUBERT MIDDLETON, who was then the manager of Holmfirth Valley Picture House and had been the first attendant of Ravensknowle Museum. Walter, Marion and Gertrude did not receive payment for being Bamforth child models, but were given sets of photographs. If Frank Bamforth required a smiling Gertrude he sent for Alf Foy, who used to stand on his head.

JESUS HIGH IN GLORY (2).

| Though Thou art so holy, | Thou wilt stoop to listen, |
| Heaven's Almighty King, | When Thy praise we sing. |

ANNIE HINCHLIFFE, centre, probably in the local church for this series of hymns. The child to her immediate right could be Marion Leake. Frank Bamforth was organist and choirmaster at Little Magnum church. He enlisted some of his choir girls for the hymn and song cards. Religious festivals prompted the production of commemorative cards such as this.

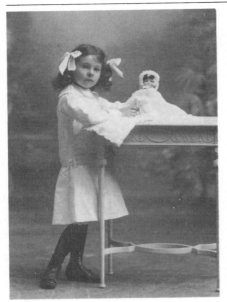

KATHLEEN CROWTHER, of Primrose Hill, with her doll in around 1917. 'Best' dolls, like best clothes, used often to be brought out only on special occasions. Not every family could afford to take Dolly to a dolls' hospital. Oh, what consternation there was when another little girl lost 'Mary Anne'. All day long she was searched for, then found dusty and forlorn in a corner of the garden, having been shaken out with the pegged rug that morning.

BLIND MAN'S BUFF.
"I KNOW—IT'S TEACHER!"

WHAT FUN HOLMFIRTH CHILDREN HAD posing for Bamforth's postcards. If the sun was shining and conditions were suitable one of the Bamforth family would pop into Holmfirth National School and select the child, or children required. Janey Bamforth's concert parties were held in Holmfirth Drill Hall, today the Civic Hall. Later on there were matinées, with Charlie Senior tinkling out tunes to accompany silent films. Charlie took sporadic bites from a 2½d. pork pie, bought from Turner Mattrick's pork butchers, while playing.

MARION LEAKE. Remember what it was like being too small to reach the wash-basin? Marion, when Mrs Barrowclough, lived on Wakefield Road, Dalton, until her death. Her many photographs of herself when a child live on in Holmfirth Postcard Museum, and in many people's albums. She recorded the song 'Daddy' in her later years, as a souvenir of the early days sitting on her father's knee at Bamforth's posing for the song set. To make those little 'bob' curls Marion's hair was washed with soft soap from a tin. Then her mother twisted her daughter's hair round soft rags.

IT WAS EVER SO! Marion Leake and Harry Marshall on the garden seat, while an envious 'outsider' looks on. Edwin Bamforth had, by this time, hit on the idea of producing postcards from existing lantern slides, depicting the popular songs of the day. Almost immediately offices had to be opened in London and New York to cope with the demand. Between 1908 and 1914 the firm flirted briefly with the notion of producing comedy films and was one of the earliest pioneers of motion pictures.

TWO'S COMPANY, THREE'S NONE.

PHILIP AND HAZEL TAYLOR in 1929 on an ornate, but not very comfortable, *chaise-longue* of the period. A black horsehair sofa was to be avoided at all costs, unless a cloth was thrown over it, for it was like sitting on a hedgehog. Sunday evenings at Grandma's were spent playing ludo and snakes and ladders, and looking at a box of photographs and black edged memorial cards. When the gas lamps flickered and dulled, Grandma pulled some chains and it brightened again. We listened to *Children's Hour* on the wireless, and were allowed one liquorice torpedo every time the clock chimed the hour.

A GROUP OF SCHOOLCHILDREN in a Cowlersley field in the 1920s. It looks like Arnold Hoyle seated on the front row. Remember those days of ink monitors, when one selected child could go round filling the inkwells in the desks?

BRYAN COOKE AND TOY CAR. Who would have thought that those tiny 'Dinkie' cars children used to find in their Christmas stockings during the thirties would now be collectors items?

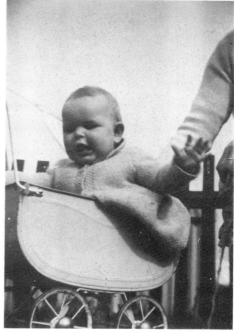

NOT QUITE SMALL ENOUGH TO FIT INTO A PINT POT, but just able to squeeze into a doll's pram. Caroline Wheeler at Crosland Moor (Thornleigh Road) in 1957. Caroline now of Yiewsley, near London, was presented with her long service medal from the Special Constabulary last year.

PHILIP TAYLOR trying out Uncle Kenneth's motor cycle at Flemminghouse Lane, Waterloo, in the 1930s. The obsession of the day was collecting cigarette cards of sporting celebrities and film stars. In 1937 a packet of Senior Service cigarettes cost sixpence for ten, and a shilling for twenty. Some children went to Saturday matinées at cinemas even if it was a scorching summer day. Rin-Tin-Tin was a hero of many. Bing Crosby was at the Empire, Huddersfield, in *Pennies From Heaven,* also starring Madge Evans, in the week of 9 May.

GRANVILLE WHEELER AND TWIN SISTER MARGARET in shorts on the lawn at 11 Lowestwood, Bargate, Linthwaite in 1938. Many old houses were similarly covered with ivy. Shorts were a novelty, little girls having usually worn dresses up until then.

YOUNG CAROLINE AND ELIZABETH WHEELER blowing dandelion clocks on wasteland in front of Avison Road, Cowlersley. Trousers were a rarity for little girls before the 1960s. Heywoods in Huddersfield sold smart children's coats in the January sale in 1959 – Caroline had one costing 28s., and Elizabeth's with a velvet collar, cost 30s. It was the time of *Andy Pandy*, *The Woodentops* and *Sooty* on children's TV. As we did not have a set Grandma, at Avison Road, was visited regularly in the afternoons.

END OF TERM AT DALTON JUNIOR SCHOOL. Katherine Abbot with her clutch of games waits to cross the Wakefield Road in 1965. Peter Meal was teaching at Dalton Junior and Miss Patterson was headmistress. At this time family allowance was 8s. for the second child, none for the first. Mary Taylor taught piano at Rowland Avenue, Dalton. Alec Fiddes was in charge of school crossing patrols. Huddersfield children were still taking the 11-plus examination and tying door knobs to drainpipes with string on Mischief Night.

DALTON JUNIOR SCHOOL GIRLS enjoying a birthday party in the woods and fields by Oaklands Old People's Home in the early 1960s. From left to right: Caroline Wheeler, -?-, Elizabeth Wheeler, -?-, -?-, Kathy Harling, -?-, Lynn Hirst, Jane Dalby and Lisa McCargo.

GOOD NIGHT !

BAMFORTH MODEL, MARION LEAKE. After lunch on Christmas Day the Leake family walked to Marion's great uncle Alfred's farm at Austenley, near the Isle of Skye public house, making sure they reached home again before early dusk. After a scrumptious tea everyone contributed to the evening's entertainment. Marion played the violin and her father always requested 'The Christmas Hymn' for her party piece.

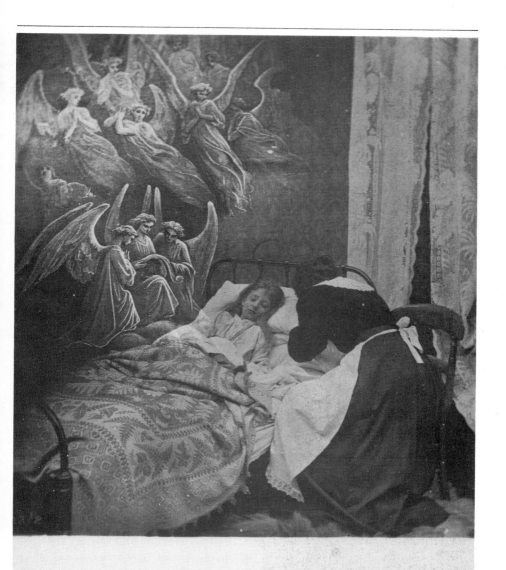

ABIDE WITH ME.

MARION LEAKE was one of the first child models for Bamforth's of Holmfirth, in the years before the war. She was given threepence every time she posed for a postcard, from 1904 until 1910. Her father worked in a quarry, walking there four miles, and back again after work. Many a time he was roped in for a bit of play acting too, in his working clothes. Syndey earned $3\frac{1}{2}$d. an hour toiling in Newgate Quarry. When Marion's brother died from scarlet fever, the house had to be fumigated and until that was done none of the family were allowed to mingle with others. They walked over the moors until it was finished.

ACKNOWLEDGEMENTS

My grateful thanks are due to the following for their help in making possible this second volume of photographs concerning Huddersfield faces and places:

Mr John O'Hara • Mr and Mrs Tom Jessop • Mr Bryan Cooke
Mr Kenneth Cousins • Mrs Edith Walker • Mrs Mary Clark • Mr James Ainley
Mr Ronnie Booth • Mrs Barbara Dvorskyj • Mrs Betty Swales
Miss Dorothy Atha • Mrs Dorothy Suthers • Mr and Mrs Jack Firth
Mrs Harriet Bailey • Mrs Ada Marston • Mrs W. Halstead
Mr Norman Wilkinson (for kindly lending a book) • Mrs Margaret Hawkins
Mr Colman Flaherty • Mr & Mrs John Carter • Mrs Muriel Kelly
E. Beaumont (opticians) • Bamforth of Holmfirth • the *Huddersfield Examiner*
Bray's photographers, Holmfirth • the staff of Huddersfield Public Library local history and Archives.
Thanks also to Mr Alan Bird who gave me the photographs of Woodhouse church and the old Co-operative Stores which he found in an antique fair in Berkshire!